Thinking about Thinking

Herman Veitch

Published by Herman Veitch, 2017.

THINKING ABOUT THINKING

First edition. December 13, 2017.

ISBN: 979-8224287826

Written by Herman Veitch.

Table of Contents

THINKING ABOUT THINKING
An Introduction to Observing your own mind
Herman Veitch

Thank you for reading. If you enjoy this book, please leave a review.

Cover design by Kevin Lucas
Copy editing by Dorian Haarhoff
Proofreading by Anne Haarhoff

Foreword

Blink 1

"Happiness is the result of a life well lived."
—Carol Ryff

In a word:
Introduction

The Tweet:
This book is an introduction to observing our thinking. We focus on the practical and useful application of popular scientific findings to create our happiness.

The Post:

- This text is for people who want to transform from surviving to thriving.

- It is aimed at readers that want to make sense of their world in a meaningful way.

- Behind the themes introduced here are vast fields to explore.

- The invitation is to explore them and leave the introduction behind as childhood is left behind.

- Beautiful complex concepts are presented simply so that these can be used in everyday life.

- The content is a summary of a decade's experience with coaching clients.

- Useful memes, thinking tools, and models that form a repeated pattern are presented.

• Read the Blinks for a quick overview and the content to understand more deeply.

Since 2006 I have enjoyed the privilege of being present with a good number of individuals as they transformed their lives. They moved from stuck mundane surviving to exhilarating optimal thriving. I picture this experience as me sitting in the shade of a tree, and as people's journeys cross mine, they join me in the shade out of the burning sun. This represents their current situation. Together we spend significant moments as they allow me to think with them about the meaningfulness of their lives and the direction of their purpose. As they leave after the brief rest in the shade, they walk away with a confident step, believing in their strength.

I hope this book will reach more of those people who want to transform from living a pauper's life to that of royalty. It is written for those who have had enough of being stuck and want to fly with the strength of their wings.

I see this book as an introduction. An introduction to the reader's ability to start creating positive change for themselves. Behind the themes discussed here are vast fields to explore. I encourage you to explore beyond this book. Hopefully this introduction can then be left behind as childhood is left behind. I often refer to authors and books that I suggest you read. These books give more detailed descriptions of the concepts discussed. Their authors have influenced my opinions. I hope that by reading them you can be further enriched.

I also tend to simplify beautiful complex concepts. Bear with me, please. I know I leave out stuff. My intent is to make the concepts useful. A significant moment in my life formed this drive for useful concepts. I spent two years in Belgium where I worked with a roof layer. I was just out of university and freely shared with him my theories on how life is supposed to be. The roof layer, also named Herman, asked me: "But how are you going to apply this in your life?" I could not answer him, and from this question sprung my drive to find practical usefulness for my theories.

So be assured that what I share in this book I have applied in my life. I also own up to the way I've presented the concepts. According to how Herman sees and experiences the world. My expectation is that you will go beyond my viewpoint. Use it as a starting point for your journey in which you come to know your world more intimately.

In the past decade, working with my Business and Life Coaching clients in co-creating their vision, I have noticed an emerging pattern. In one way or another they have found value in the stories, tools, and arguments I shared. I offer this pattern in the book.

Although I try and make the argument flow logically with the simple and powerful ABC think tool, you might follow a different sequence. In the chaos of life some elements make sense and are relevant at different times in your life. Use as appropriate.

Please see this book as a coaching conversation that introduces you to your thinking. These concepts made a difference in the lives of my clients; I hope they do so for you, the reader, as well.

I have structured the book simply, trying to be as succinct as possible. AT the start of each argument, I placed a blink. The blink will give you a compact overview. You can then read the content of each chapter. The Introduction is about the foundational departure point and the core ABC thinking tool. In six chapters I discuss the three elements of the ABC thinking and expand them with other thinking tools. If you feel something is missing, please explore by reading the recommended books or feel free to contact me. I would love to explore further with you.

On a more personal level, I wrote this book, mostly, lest I forget. I have always been a bit absentminded, but recently I have realized that I am starting to forget valuable lessons. Writing helps me remember and I hope that by remembering I can be of value to you.

I acknowledge sources of information as far as I can, but some elude me. Where I have not acknowledged accurately, I apologize. Perhaps you can direct me to the right source.

"Happiness is the result of a life well lived." —Carol Ryff

Chapter 1

Introduction

Blink 2

"Knowing is not enough; we must apply. Willing is not enough; we must do."

—Johann Wolfgang von Goethe

In a word:

Happiness

The Tweet:

Happiness is life's ultimate goal no matter how we define it. Your definition of success deserves a closer look. Does it make you happy?

The Post:

- Linking success, happiness, and action.

- Each one of us wants our life to be meaningful.

- The expectation is that this meaningful success will bring us happiness.

- Success is not something that comes on its own; it is created through action.

- Not all action leads to success.

- Our happiness depends on the quality of our actions.

- The quality of our action is determined by the quality of our thinking about the action.

- Action is behavior that can be summarized on a continuum.

- Our genes dictate 50% of our behavior.

- Of the other 50%, 10% is our conditioning, and 40% comprises of the choices we make.

- Most people are on autopilot and only live up to 60% of their capacity.

- You want to live intentionally at 100% of your capacity.

Everybody wants to be successful. Each one of us pursues an experience of achieving something worthwhile. We define what that something is in a million ways. And no matter what that definition is, the expectation is that this will bring us happiness. To be happy (successful) is a normal human pursuit.

Happiness is, therefore, the ultimate goal.[1]

To be happy and successful we must know one thing. Successful living depends on your taking action. Success is not something that comes on its own; we create it. We can dream of success, but it is only when we act that we shift the boundaries of our world to include the desired happiness. What you do makes you successful.

Not all action leads to success. It is also true that all of us are busy in one way or another, but not necessarily happy because of what we do. If that were so, the whole world would be happy. As human beings, we easily fall into the trap of busyness and chase our tails. Many people tread the proverbial hamster wheel, running but not getting anywhere. How then can action open up happiness? And how does this action differ from the one on the hamster wheel?

The answer is simply that the quality of the action counts. The quality of our action is determined by the quality of our thinking about the action.[2]

To pursue actions that result in your success we need to look at your thinking about your actions. This is at the heart of this book.

Thinking about your thinking (about the quality of your actions). We will use the boomerang effect. Seemingly throw our attention in the wrong direction, but eventually, we will hit the target, and the benefits will return into our hands.

Action is behavior and can be placed on a continuum. Let's say the whole of the continuum makes up 100%.

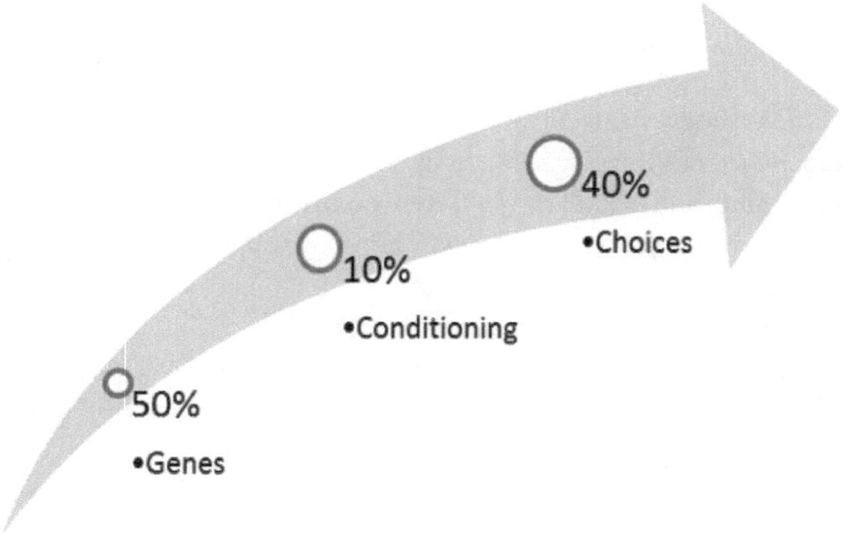

Figure 1 - Behavioral continuum

Our genes dictate 50% of our behavior. I am not referring to those genes that dictate the color of your hair or eyes. I am referring to the genes that drive behavior.

These behavior-driving genes are an object of numerous scientific studies. We can assume that the last words have not yet been spoken, so for our conversation I would like to keep things simple. Genes are the fundamental building blocks of being human and are responsible for all base behavior. Base behavior is all behavior that leads to survival of the species. We could categorize this behavior into three behavioral agenda points. At the most basic level we humans are concerned with three Fs: Food (What will I eat?), Fear (Will I be safe?) and Fornication (With whom can I procreate?). These three agendas might sound simplistic, but they present in subtle and complex ways. Why do you think beautiful models are used to sell anything from cars to Caribbean holidays?

Ten percent is our conditioning. Conditioning is everything you know up to this point in time. All your experiences, everything your parents and school teachers have taught you. All the socially acceptable behavior promoted by your culture, government or media. Everything you have figured out for yourself, everything, even part of your personality, is captured in this 10%. It is huge.

Now turn around and look at the vastness of the 40% left to choice.

Most people live using up to 60% of their capacity. They are driven by their genetic base behavior agenda, and they address these agendas through their conditioning. They are on autopilot. They do not question why things are what they are; they just carry on.

You are reading this book because you want to play in the 40% field of potentiality. You are tired of only dreaming of your happiness. You want to change and be successful. You want to live by choice, intention and design. At 100% of your capacity. Welcome to the journey that few people are willing to take.

"Knowing is not enough; we must apply. Willing is not enough; we must do."
—*Johann Wolfgang von Goethe*

Blink 3

We are what we repeatedly do. Excellence, then, is not an act, but a habit." —Aristotle

In a word:

Your Brain

The Tweet:

The brain in all its beautiful complexity can be understood through a few simple principles. This helps to explore the quality of our thinking to improve the quality of our actions.

The Post:

- It is beneficial to spend time understanding how our brain works.

- The brain constantly connects new information to old information.

- It has pre-existing knowledge files that filter how the world is supposed to work.

- These files are like thousands of maps connecting so that we can function effectively in our world.

- These connecting maps build up our belief systems that make up the 10% conditioning.

- The brain operates on two levels: the subconscious conditioning and the conscious choice level.

- The brain is energy sensitive and quickly saves routine tasks to the conditioning level.

- Routine tasks become habits that drive our success regardless of our awareness of them.

- We all are on autopilot until we choose to become aware of our thoughts.

How the brain works

If the quality of our actions is determined by the quality of our thinking it will be beneficial to know how our thinking tool works. So let us spend some time understanding our brain a little better.

The brain in all its beautiful complexity can be understood through a few simple principles. One of its main functions is to make sense of the world. Our brain constantly takes the input we receive through our senses and files the information in pre-existing knowledge 'files.' These files are like mental maps (hardwired neurological connections or interpretation filters) of how the world is supposed to work.

For everything we encounter we have a preconceived construct that helps us understand what is supposed to happen next. Thousands of these maps connect in order for us to function effectively in our world and these connecting maps build up our belief systems, that is, the complex and intricate system of how we believe the world is supposed to work.[3]

These interconnected belief systems make up the 10% conditioning through which we perceive and make sense of the world. This is an important point for the rest of our argument. What I would like to emphasize is that our conditioning consists of physical, biological connections in our mind. Much like the motherboard of a computer. It just has more flexibility and plasticity than a motherboard.

It will help to know that the brain seems to operate on two levels: working memory and long-term memory, or conscious and unconscious, or System 1 and System 2 thinking.[4] On our continuum it is the 10% conditioning and the 40% choice distinction.

Because our working memory is so energy intensive the brain either throws away chunks of information not relevant or saves information to the long-term memory as quickly as possible. Take for example learning how to drive a car. In the beginning, we have to concentrate on different things — check the rearview mirror, watch the road, pay attention to what the other drivers are doing, and use the indicators. Once we've mastered the ability to drive, we do all these things without thinking about them. The repeated action has hardwired the habit into our unconscious. Now there is free space in our working memory to attend to other relevant concerns. All automatic behavior is created and works in this way. From tying your shoes to the anger you feel when someone swears at you.

The brain uses the working memory to pay attention to what is happening in our immediate surroundings. This working memory has a small capacity (four chunks of information)[5] while using vast quantities of brain energy.

Your working memory is like a TV show with only room for four actors on the set. Ideally only two. Pay attention next time when you watch your favorite sitcom. Most sitcoms never have more than two actors interacting at a time. Our brain is wired in the same way. Ideally, we can only pay effective attention to one or two concepts at a time. If you have been in a TV or film studio while they are shooting a program you will know that they use an array of lights. Our working memory also uses a huge amount of energy to function.

Why do we need to know this? Understanding that we are driven by our habits (conditioning) and how the process of habit formation works, helps us change them. This whole process is useful. Habit formation is good for survival. We do not want to constantly think of breathing. We like it that we breathe automatically. Yet we can become aware of our breathing when we meditate and slow it down or take deeper breaths. We exist on autopilot until we choose to become aware of our thoughts. And this is the crux of thinking about our thinking: Mastering the skill of observing our thoughts.

Once a thought pattern or thinking habit has been observed it can be adapted. Hopefully, this adaption will improve the quality of that thought pattern, and through the improved thinking our behavior improves.

"We are what we repeatedly do. Excellence, then, is not an act, but a habit." —Aristotle

Blink 4

"Much of what we call emotion is nothing more or less than a certain kind — a biased, prejudiced, or strongly evaluative — kind of thought."
—Albert Ellis

In a word:
ABCD

The Tweet:
The sequence is: B interprets A, then B generates C, and C then drives D.

The Post:

• Most people think that when something happens, it creates a consequence.

• What actually happen is our belief systems (B) interpret an activating event (A).

• Our belief system (B) then creates the consequence (C) that we experience.

• The consequence energizes and directs our next action/ deed (D).

• We can find the B–C connection effective or ineffective. Keep it or change it.

• Please note right and wrong vs effective and ineffective choice of words.

• This assumes inherent authority.

So how do we go about doing this?
By using the ABC thinking tool.
Adding the D = ABCD. An acronym that stands for:

A- Activating Event
B- Belief System
C- Consequences
D- Deeds

This tool is derived from one that Albert Ellis, a well-known psychologist in the 20th century, used in his work. Let me explain how this thinking tool works.

Most people think that when something happens (activating event) it creates a consequence. This assumption is true only in the most simplistic of mechanical activities. I flick a switch, and the light comes on. For the rest of life, it is inadequate, especially when it comes to human behavior.

What happens actually is there is an activating event (A) that gets interpreted by our belief systems (B). Our belief system then creates the consequence (C) that we experience, and the consequence energizes our next action/deed (D).

The sequence is B interprets A, B then generates C, and C then drives D.

Illustrative story

Two brothers go and visit their grandparents on the farm. One night there is a heavy thunderstorm. Granny goes to see if the boys are okay. She finds one of them underneath the bed, pillow over his head, shivering with fear. She consoles him and asks why he is so afraid. "I am afraid the clouds will eat me," he says. "Listen how their tummy rumbles from hunger."

She looks for his brother and finds him sitting in front of the window. Every time the lightning flashes, he smiles from ear to ear. "Are you not afraid?" she asks. "No," he answers,

"Grandpa told me that every time the lighting flashes, God is taking pictures of his children."

The same activating event for the two boys, a thunderstorm. But two different consequences. All based on the interpretation of the activating event.

It is the B-C connection that we need to observe. If we find it effective we leave it as is. If we find it ineffective, we change it.

Allow me to pause here, to emphasize two important points:

1. Note my choice of words. I label the belief system as effective or ineffective. Not wrong or right. Let us refrain from making a value judgment. We complicate and taint the observation with moral conditioning when we judge our thinking in this way. This judgment will prevent us from moving forward constructively. Moral judgment comes later. For now, we merely need to observe and evaluate if B is effective or not. Meaning, it is effective when B gives us the consequence we want, or not.

2. Secondly, notice the assumption behind this concept. It assumes that you have the power and authority to decide what C must be. Later we will talk more about agency and autonomy that underpins this assumption of authority. For now, I want you to notice that from the start when we observe our thinking, we do so from the 40% platform of choice.

"Much of what we call emotion is nothing more or less than a certain kind — a biased, prejudiced, or strongly evaluative kind — of thought."
—Albert Ellis

Blink 5

"Life isn't about finding yourself. Life is about creating yourself."
—*George Bernard Shaw*

In a word:

Focus

The Tweet:

Observing our thoughts enables us to know what we focus on.

The Post:

• What we focus on or pay attention to determines our state of mind.

• You have the choice to focus on five levels:

1. What do you want?

2. How do you get what you want?

3. What do you need to DO to get what you want?

4. Why don't you get what you want?

5. Whose fault is it that you do not get what you want?

• Thinking about your thinking starts with your ability to observe your thoughts.

• If you don't change your mind once in a while, you are not using it.

Why is this important to observe your thoughts? What value does it have?

Hopefully you will gain valuable insights into the benefits of observing your thinking as you read this book. For now, I would like to highlight one specific value add. By observing our thoughts we become aware of what we focus on. What we focus on or pay attention to determines our state of mind. Simply put, the repeated input strengthens the neurological connection we make about the object or theme that holds our attention. It is like adding wood to a fire. The more wood, the bigger the fire. You get more of what you pay attention to. In his book *Quiet Leadership* David Rock shares a thinking tool: Five levels of focus. Five fires that we can stoke: Vision, Planning, Detail, Problems and Drama. We can translate these levels to five questions that you can use to direct your attention.

1. Vision: What do you want? In any given situation, decide what you want the outcome to be. This helps you to be proactive. Knowing what you want can be as simple as "I want a cup of coffee," or it can be your ultimate life vision. Be clear about the desired result and focus on it. Dream your dreams, have your vision. We all need something strong to pull us away from our current situation.

2. Planning: How do you get what you want? Having a dream is of no use if you do not have a plan to realize it. So sit down and make a plan to get to your desired result. Write it down. Don't just think about it. The act of writing is the first minuscule step to realizing the plan. People assume they will remember it. Unfortunately our memories are not as reliable as we think. Write down your plan; you can always change it later.

3. Detail: What do you need to DO to get what you want? This is the action part. Do something! Dreaming and planning will get you nowhere. Remember it is the act, the first step that shifts the boundary, not the talking or the wishing. But beware of this focus area. It is easy to fall into the detail trap of busyness. If your actions are not connected

to your vision you will be busy the whole day, but have nothing to show for it. You will be chasing your tail.

4. Problems: Why don't you get what you want? This question focuses on all the problems and obstacles you place in your way. Let's face it, there are always problems. There will always be a reason for not getting what you want. An excuse. But you don't have to pay attention to it. You do not need to add fuel to this fire; it is hot enough. Focusing on problems generates more problems. I am not talking about real life troubleshooting when a system is obviously malfunctioning. Then we need to know why and solve the problem. What I am referring to here is the attitude of not taking responsibility for your life and living with rationalizations and excuses. Please do not give away your power.

5. Drama: Whose fault is it that you do not get what you want? Blame shifting. We all know people who attribute their unhappiness to other people or situations. Their failures are always some external person or factor's fault. Their lives seem to be in constant drama as they move from one tragedy to another. Don't focus your attention here. It will only pull you down to wallow in the mud of despair.

The parable of the two wolves[6]

A young Cherokee is brought before the tribal elders because they are concerned about his aggressive tendencies. One of the elders takes the young man aside and tells him that his anger is understandable since all humans have within them two wolves. One wolf is good and peaceful, and the other is evil and angry. The two wolves are in constant battle with one another since neither is powerful enough to destroy the other.

The young man asks the elder, "But if they are of equal power, which wolf will win?"

And the elder replies, "The one you feed the most."

The skill of observing our thoughts enables us to identify which fire is burning the brightest. If we like the drama in our life, throw more wood on that fire. Just know that if you feed the fire, you have to face the heat. I suggest we keep our attention on the first three levels. Feed the wolf that brings the desired happiness. Later we will talk more about your ability to take the initiative and create the life you want. For now, the point I am making is that you have the ability to choose the consequence you want and to get it. You need to take responsibility to change your belief system. B creates C and you are the artist that molds B.

In summary: Thinking about your thinking starts with your ability to observe your thoughts. Once you have observed them, you can improve their quality to give you the desired result. In the next chapter, we will take a closer look at some of the core belief systems that we can use to leverage the most useful changes. If you don't change your mind once in a while, you are not using it.

"Life isn't about finding yourself. Life is about creating yourself."
—*George Bernard Shaw*

Chapter 2

Belief Systems

Blink 6

"If I have seen further it is by standing on the shoulders of giants." —Isaac Newton

In a word:

Belief Systems

The Tweet:

Smart people have done some heavy lifting for us, and we can tap into their insights to take our thinking to the next level.

The Post:

• There are common thinking patterns that are present in the majority of people's thinking.

• The three major ineffective patterns we need to be aware of are:

1. We tend to think in terms of permanence

2. We tend to make things personal

3. Our thoughts tend to be pervasive

• It is safe to say that the effective thinking pattern is exactly the opposite:

1. Everything changes

2. Nothing is personal

3. Everything is just one thing at a time

Understanding Belief Systems

Let us explore the next level of thinking about our thinking. In this chapter I would like us to understand generally present belief systems. We'll explore five dimensions where we can improve the quality of our thinking.

Luckily for us we are not the first ones to think about our thinking. Some smart people have done heavy lifting for us, and we examine their insights here.

Martin Seligman's books *Learned Optimism*[7] and *Authentic Happiness*[8] are highly recommended. He and some other great thinkers identified common thinking patterns that are present in the majority of people's thinking. These thinking patterns are like background software that runs automatically unless we stop and change them.

Seligman gives us three major ineffective patterns we need to be aware of first:

1. Permanence: We tend to think things will go on forever, but everything always changes. We pick up on the permanence pattern when we use words like "You are always late" or "You never loved me."

2. Personal: We tend to make things personal. We think we are the center of the universe and that every little thing has a direct connection with us. Now this type of thinking is normal for a two-year-old. A two-year-old child's developmental task is to realize that the world does not revolve around them, and that a legitimate bigger world exists outside their frame of reference. Unfortunately, many adults never develop past this point.

3. Pervasive: We also tend to overgeneralize. We assume that when one thing is true for one situation, it will be true for

another. Stereotypes and biases are these thinking patterns on steroids. Normally it is a negative effect that we allow to spill over, and we go into a new situation with preconceived ideas of what should be. We miss the beauty of what is.

There are other thinking patterns such as catastrophizing and black-and-white thinking, but these three are the most common ineffective patterns. What then would effective patterns look like? Well basically the exact opposite:

1. Nothing is permanent. Everything changes. We are part of ever-evolving nature. Even the sun will stop shining at some time, and atoms constantly flicker in and out of existence, but we humans tend to deny this truth of ever-present flux. I find a rare gift in constant change. Embracing that everything changes, I know that when things are going badly, I just need to keep going because the bad times will change. And when things are going well, I need to pay attention and savor every moment, because good times also change and don't last. This helps me to have hope in bad times and motivates me to say "I love you" or "Thank you" when I am in harmony.

2. One of my most liberating moments was when I realized that "Nothing anybody says or does is because of me" (Don Miguel Ruiz's *Four Agreements*).[9] In our adolescence we tend to be concerned about what others think about us. This is okay because we are busy forming our identity. When we reach young adulthood we do not care what others think about us; we are trying to make our unique mark in the world. Then when we reach maturity we realize people do not think about us, they mostly think only about

themselves. Nothing is personal until we choose to make it so.

"An insult can only be given where it is taken." —*CJ Langenhoven*

Let me explain this truth through the use of our ABC thinking tool.

Scenario 1:

I am wearing my favorite sweater. You compliment me on it, "What a nice sweater." I feel good about it.

The activating event is your compliment, my belief system a positive connection with the sweater, and my consequence a warm, feel-good "Thank you for the compliment." My positive response is your activating event, filtered through your positive belief system and your consequence is a smile.

Scenario 2:

I am wearing the same sweater, but it is the last clean sweater in the cupboard, and it is scratching my neck. You compliment me on it, "What a nice sweater." I respond, "This old thing. Don't be sarcastic."

Again the activating event is your comment, but because my belief system is negative toward the sweater, you receive a dismissal. My dismissal becomes your activating event and so on.

Nothing anybody says or does is because of you. People say or do because of their belief systems that interpret our actions or words.

3. Everything is just one thing. We will make life easier for ourselves when we learn this truth. Yes, everything is connected, and we will share a conversation about this later. But for now, we need to know everything is just one thing. In this moment, all I am doing is typing these words. All you are doing is reading them. There is only the now.

There is a story of a troubled king. A beggar gives him a ring and urges him to turn it around on his finger when distressed. The king reads the words written on the ring: This too will pass.

In the most difficult times of my life being present has saved me many times. I can remember a specific high stake negotiation that went well because I could be present with the other person and did not dwell on the consequences. Be here now. Not in the future or in the past. Just here. Breathe and savor the moment. Everything is just one thing. It's a phone call. A conversation. A question. Do not attach speculative outcomes to the act. Just do the one thing. Then the next one and then the next. Be present in each act, and you will find yourself moving forward with much less stress.

Someone asked a friend, whose guru had recently died, what she enjoyed doing most. The answer was whatever she was doing at the moment.

"If I have seen further it is by standing on the shoulders of giants." —Isaac Newton[10]

Blink 7

If you are going in the right direction, all you need to do is put one foot in front of the other." —Dalai Lama

In a word:

Movement

The Tweet:

Our brain moves away from threats and toward rewards. Placing this movement on a normal distribution curve helps us manage the movement.

The Post:

• Our brain moves away from that which threatens it, and it moves toward that which rewards it.

• The human brain is wired for "error detection" as well as "solution generation."

• The normal distribution curve is a handy thinking tool.

• It simply says in any population half will act in a certain way and the other half not.

• It is a dynamic continuum with no fixed point.

• The brain's "toward" and "away" movement can effectively be placed on this continuum.

• Relevant research has gone into identifying five dimensions that demonstrate "away" and "toward" movements:

1. Our self-esteem and social status

2. Our need for consistency and certainty

3. Our sense of agency

4. Our sense of belonging

5. Our sense of justice

How our brain moves

David Rock will also help us think about our thinking. In *Your Brain at Work* [11] he shares with us his SCARF model, a handy and versatile thinking tool to use. It summarizes research into the SCARF acronym which stands for Status, Certainty, Autonomy, Relatedness and Fairness. Concepts we'll explore in the next few chapters.

His understanding is that our brain, in all its beautiful complexity, works simply. It moves away from that which threatens it, and it gravitates toward that which rewards it. Not rocket science, is it? But it has a surprising depth. Allow me to share some of this depth.

Another way to look at the "toward" and "away" movement is to add the perspective of the psychiatrist Alfred Adler. He stated that half of the population sees the world as a safe place and the other half sees the world as a dangerous one. This is informed by the way adults took care of us as infants. In adults we see this difference in emphasis when we distinguish between pessimists and optimists.

Most people see the optimist as better than the pessimist. I invite you to reconsider this assumption. The optimist created the airplane and the pessimist the parachute. We need both.

The human brain is wired for "error detection" as well as "solution generation." To explain these two functions, let's jump back in time and observe our ancestors on the plains of Africa. Those who picked up on the error that that dark patch does not belong under that bush survived the lion stalking them. Those who did not notice the error became lunch.

Those ancestors that climbed a tree or ran away to solve the problem of being stalked survived. Those who noticed the error and did nothing also became supper.

You and I are descendants of those who survived. We have both the ability to detect errors and to find solutions. The challenge is that error detection is our default mode. We easily see what is wrong. The solution mode must deliberately be activated. This takes effort but most people are too lazy to take the time to think of a solution.

As you can see, this "away" and "toward" movement has locked within itself a few jewels. The normal distribution curve is a useful tool to uncover these jewels.

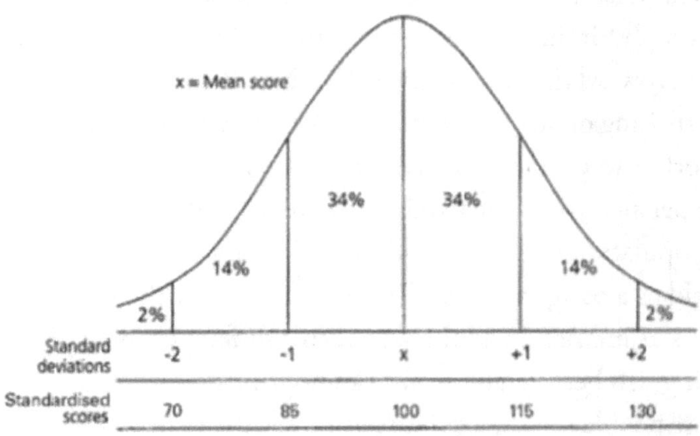

Fig 2 – Normal distribution

The normal distribution curve comes from the world of statistics and research. Simply put, it shows in any population that half of the population will act in a certain way and the other half not. It is a handy thinking tool if you keep in mind that it is never fixed, but a dynamic continuum.

It has a median (normally X/0) or if you like an average: 50% of any population will be above average, and 50% will be below average.

What makes it useful is that it places the exceptions to the rule in the 2% at the top and the bottom of the scale

Let us take IQ as an example. The normal distribution says that if the average IQ is 120, half of the population will be above average and half will be below average: 2% will be geniuses, and 2% will be seriously intellectually impaired. The rest of us fall somewhere in the 34% and 14 % on both sides of the median.

Let's apply the normal distribution to the broader population in contexts of our deeper understanding of the "toward" and "away" movement. We can assume that half of the population's departure point is from an error detection point. They tend to be pessimistic, think the world is dangerous, and easily find fault. But remember, this is a continuum and constantly dynamic. This half only needs to apply more effort to find the solution. Of this half, 2% are unmovable in their negativity, 14% are stuck in their ways and will change with great difficulty, but 34% see the error. This acts as a warning signal for the human race that we need to fix that which is not working.

The other half of the normal distribution consists of solution generators. They are optimistic and see the world as a safe place: 2% of them live in la-la land, 14% tend to be naïve and are dreamers, and 34% create solutions to the errors that the pessimist presents to them.

And here is the best part of this whole argument: Each one of us has both tendencies in us. Applying this tool in our thinking about our thinking we can assume that in any given time frame, 50% of our thinking is in a "toward" state or is solution focused. We feel the world is a safe place, and 50% of the time our brain is in an "away" state or in error detection mode. This feels the world is dangerous. Now that we know this we can move up and down the continuum. We are all capable of so much more than that which our conditioning dictates.

Moving sounds easy enough, but life can be complicated. So let's break this rich "toward" and "away" movement down into the five sub-movements. Sub-movements that are belief systems or mental maps generally present in human behavior.

Relevant research has gone into identifying these five "away" and "toward" movements in our brain. We will discuss them in more detail. They are:

1. Our need for consistency and certainty
2. Our sense of agency
3. Our sense of belonging
4. Our self-esteem and social status
5. Our sense of justice

In the next two chapters we will explore our thinking about these five movements. We will first focus on what I see as the core movements — Consistency, Agency, and Belonging. In Chapter 4 we will then think through status and justice.

If you are going in the right direction, all you need to do is put one foot in front of the other."
—Dalai Lama

Chapter 3

Consistency, Agency, and Belonging

Blink 8

"When you recognize uncertainty, you recognize that you may be able to influence the outcomes. Hope is an embrace of the unknown and the unknowable, an alternative to the certainty of both optimists and the pessimists." —Rebecca Solnit

In a word:

Consistency

The Tweet:

A paradox is when we have to entertain two opposing ideas and allow them to co-exist in the same space. Our need for consistency and constant change is such a paradox.

The Post:

- We have to contain and maintain two important truths in our mind. Consistency and Change.

- Everything changes.

- Having certainty is important for our wellbeing.

- Losing the illusion of permanence and being safe enough asks for a serious reframing of our minds.

- Knowing the difference between commitment and attachment helps.

- The normal distribution thinking tool also helps us deal with this paradox.

- Few of us are competent in the skill of dealing with change.

• Because change is the only constant, developing our change muscle will add enormous value.

• Educate yourself to understand the change process.

• Change always includes a loss and therefore initiates a mourning process.

• Learn to recognize the five phases associated with mourning: Shock, Denial, Bargaining, Anger and Acceptance.

Consistency

Enter a paradox.

A paradox is when we have to entertain two opposing ideas and allow them to co-exist in the same space. The poet John Keats wrote about this state of mind "when a man is capable of being in uncertainties, mysteries, doubts, without any irritable reaching after fact and reason."

Exploring our thinking about these "toward" and "away" movements, we will need to contain two important truths in our mind: Consistency and Change.

Given our need for consistency we paradoxically oppose the truth that everything changes. Remember the ineffective thinking pattern of permanence? And that we need to embrace change as a gift? Here we will engage with both sides of the coin because both are present in our lives. So let's put our minds together and explore this paradox

I am fascinated by how we humans cling to the illusion of permanence. We pursue an eternal life in our religions and spirituality. We spend a fortune on being forever young and keeping things the same. We all move away from uncertainty and toward certainty. In my life I have realized that I am okay with variation, but that I also have a deep resistance to change. This was brought home to me when we moved from one country to another. Even though I was irritated by the over-familiarity of living in one city for 30 years, the process of detaching myself from an established support system exposed me to my squirming and dodging. I realized I had a bunch of techniques for resisting change. We dearly want things to stay the same, and we want to be certain of what will happen next. We want to feel in control of the next step. We feel that if we are in control we are safe, and being safe ensures that we survive.

Being safe enough to survive falls in the 50% gene-controlled domain. This has critical mass in our behavior drivers. So we need to pay attention to our conditioning regarding this critical mass, not to resist it or deny this illusion, but to improve our conditioning around this illusion of certainty.

We live with multiple illusions, and we need the illusion of certainty to function effectively in our world. For example, you and I may think we are staying in one place, but in reality we are moving at a speed of 66,000 miles per hour (107,000 km/hr) through space as the earth orbits the sun. We experience the same effect when we sit on a plane; it feels as if we are stationary, but we are traveling from one continent to another. Our senses would not be able to comprehend this high-speed flux so we believe the illusion that tells us things are stable. Which they are, surprisingly, as the reality collapses into our experience of it (this has to do with the complicated conversation about quantum physics[12] that we will not cover in this book).

Sufficient for us is to know we need to find a way to embrace this paradox that everything changes and stays the same at the same time. Accepting both as a reality is the healthier way to go as opposed to attaching to only one of them.

Attachment vs commitment

It helps to distinguish between attachment and commitment.

Attachment is an emotional weight we place on a single outcome. Let's say a teenager who loves tennis wants to play for the school team.

If she attaches to that one outcome, she places an emotional expectation on this outcome. If she gets into the team she is on cloud nine; if she misses the team, she is devastated.

Commitment is the dedication to a greater cause. If our teenage girl commits to the dream of playing at Wimbledon one day, then getting into the school team is just one of many outcomes en route to that great goal. Sure she will be unhappy if she does not make the school team, but because of her commitment to the bigger picture, she can bounce back more easily.

Let's use our normal distribution thinking tool to deal with this paradox. As we constantly move up and down the continuum between the two force fields of consistency and change, they pull us toward themselves. We can play around with the names of these two powers if we want to — growth and stagnation, evolution and inertia, life and death.

According to our thinking tool, we can accept that 68% of life (34% + 34% on both sides of the median) will include small changes and constancies. For example, there is a 34% chance that your doctor's appointment might change because of an emergency on the doctor's side, but also a 34% chance that the appointment will not change. We will experience big changes in 14% of our life, and 14% will seldom change (moving from one town to another or staying in the same one). We can then also expect 2% chance of major change, while 2% will remain solid and always as it was.

The same principle can be applied when we observe the people who interact with us. We can safely use the normal distribution to plot people we deal with in terms of their change resistance and change acceptance: 2% of the people will never change. They are stuck in their way, while 14% will change with great difficulty. They will show resistance and take a long time to move, and 34% will be slow to change and complain about it. The other 34% will accept change easily and

14% will be the change agents that advocate the change, and 2% are the visionaries that create the new reality.

The normal distribution helps us frame the paradox. Yet, we still need to equip ourselves to deal with change. This flexibility is a skill where few of us achieve competence. Mostly because we attach too strongly to consistency. This is understandable given the strong experience of being safe when we know what will happen next. But as we all know, change is the only constant. So how do we stretch our change muscle to become strong and flexible?

Regardless of where we are on this distribution, change will happen, and we need to equip ourselves to deal with it. Luckily there are already giants on whose shoulders we stand. I recommend reading about change and change management to enhance your skill. For now, I would like to describe a perspective on the change process.

Initially, there will be excitement about the change. Our brain likes new connections, and when something different is introduced, it pays attention. Depending where on the continuum the degree of change falls, this excitement may be short or long in duration. The length of this excitement depends on whether the change is small or major and if it is perceived as positive or negative. If it is a negative, our brain will quickly register it and then go into defense mode (away from movement). If positive change, the brain will stay fascinated for a longer period to explore the possibilities (toward movement).

Eventually, the novelty wears off, and then we go into a mourning period. Again, depending on the degree of change, this mourning period can be fleeting or stay with us for months.

What I call a mourning period is more a sense of loss. We constantly lose something. The major 2% change of losing a loved one is easy to identify and hopefully less frequent. It is the smaller 34% changes that we often miss. Not being on time for a show. Not having expectations met in a relationship. Not being invited to an event you wanted to go too. Small stuff, but we all go through the mourning process regardless of the degree of loss. The degree of loss or change merely dictates the speed we go through the mourning.

Mourning goes through well-documented phases.[13] Initially, there will be shock or surprise. Denial. We cannot believe it happened. Then we go into a bargaining phase. We try and negotiate with ourselves, other people or the spiritual powers to keep the status quo. When this does not happen, we go into a melancholic or sulking phase. We feel like doing nothing, because what is the use? Depression. Then we snap out of this miserable phase and go into an anger phase. We feel this change is unfair in many different ways.

For me, this is a sign of healing, but many people feel guilty when it happens. Some people want to deny this because their conditioning says anger is not acceptable. Or how can you be angry with your deceased loved one? But anger is positive. It generates energy to move forward, and we should embrace it. Not lock it away behind passive–aggressive tactics or self-sabotaging behaviors.

The last phase is acceptance. This is when we make peace with the change. We embrace the scars of loss as proof of a life well lived, and love lost, and start to engage with the new reality.

With the acceptance of the change the new reality becomes the status quo, and we build toward the improvement of this new reality. This last phase is a creative phase, as we engage with more experience because we are wiser and stronger. We have survived, now we can start to thrive.

Be forewarned though of two important points. First, this process is never a clear-cut step-by-step process, but rather a messy, disorganized one. The phases do not follow each other logically, and they are not evenly spaced. But you now know that there are phases. You can therefore identify and deal with them more easily. Secondly, in any change process, there are always fallbacks. You will get to a point where you find yourself saying "Not this again!" For example, when we change from a bad habit to a good habit, somewhere along the line we will fall back into the bad habit. This is normal resistance to change. Unfortunately, many people give up and start believing they cannot change and succumb to the old habit.

I invite you to change your perspective. Consider a spiral. Seen from the top, it looks like the line circles back to cross itself. Change your perspective and look at the spiral from the side and you see that the loopback is at a higher level. What you are experiencing in the change process is a normal loopback. Seemingly you are back at the same place, but in reality, you are circling at a higher level. What seems as the same old stuff is just an opportunity to learn more detail or find deeper meaning in a specific aspect of your experience.

Fig 3 – Spiral

So pay attention. You are in the process of becoming a competent expert on your life. With this open-minded attitude it is so much easier to live with the paradox of change and consistency. I think you will find yourself in a "toward" state of mind more frequently.

"When you recognize uncertainty, you recognize that you may be able to influence the outcomes. Hope is an embrace of the unknown and the unknowable, an alternative to the certainty of both optimists and pessimists." —Rebecca Solnit

Blink 9

> *"Some people feel the rain. Others just get wet."*
> —*Bob Marley*

In a word:

Agency

The Tweet:

The implication of taking responsibility for your life is simultaneously liberating and "egoclastic." It is the cornerstone for creating happiness.

The Post:

- To take up the responsibility for your life is to take up your agency.

- Your agency is you owning your ability to respond and to choose.

- This ability to choose is fundamental to your wellbeing.

- This fundamentally anchors our sense of agency in our personal authority.

- Personal authority is made up of two concepts:

1. Our locus of control – Asking the question "Who has the authority?"

2. Our locus of causality – Asking the question "From where are things caused?"

- Locus of control and causality can be either internal or external.

• The dynamic interplay between these two concepts creates four mentalities:

1. The Victim

2. The Struggler

3. The Gambler

4. The Creator

• Taking responsibility for your life also holds in itself an uncomfortable truth.

• Our external world is a reflection of our internal world.

Sense of Agency

One of the cornerstones of success is taking responsibility for your life. In my mind everything that is worthwhile and significantly good starts to happen when we make a choice: "My life is my responsibility."

Taking responsibility for your life is no small thing. The implications are staggering. It is simultaneously liberating and "egoclastic."[14] In the Greek tragedy, despite the prediction of fate, Oedipus takes responsibility for his own actions. Join me as we unpack this important choice we all need to make to safeguard our happiness.

Invictus
Out of the night, that covers me,
Black as the pit from pole to pole,
I thank whatever gods may be
For my unconquerable soul.
In the fell clutch of circumstance
I have not winced nor cried aloud.
Under the bludgeonings of chance
My head is bloody but unbowed.

Beyond this place of wrath and tears
Looms but the Horror of the shade,
And yet the menace of the years
Finds and shall find me unafraid.
I
t matters not how strait the gate,
How charged with punishments the scroll,
I am the master of my fate,
I am the captain of my soul.
- William Ernest Henley

Our knee-jerk reaction is to blame somebody or something. When you take responsibility for your life, you take up your agency. You claim your ability to respond. You become the author of your story. When we talk of your agency or your sense of agency we refer to your capacity to act independently and to intentionally influence your functioning in the course of an environmental event.

Big words that basically say you use your free will. But I do not want to reduce it to such a simple definition. There is much more to this belief system than simply having the ability to choose.

The ability to choose is fundamental to our wellbeing. If someone or a situation takes away our freedom to choose, we wither. We all strongly move away from such a context, and if you look at all the disasters happening in history, it normally has to do with people's autonomy (used here as a synonym for agency) being taken away from them. Contrast this with when we are given a choice. We are more open to people or situations. We engage more and take more ownership for what is happening. For our life and in our dealing with other people, we need to understand this concept.

Join me then in thinking about this at a deeper level. In my thinking and how I apply it in my life, I noticed that one of the fundamental belief systems anchoring my sense of agency was the belief in my authority.

The belief in our authority — the power to execute — seems to be interwoven into our sense of agency. The picture in my head is that of me being the director who determines which actor does or says what on stage. There are people who do not fully take up the directorship. They allow other people or circumstances to dictate what the actor's thoughts and/or emotions do. To become competent directors we need to explore and understand personal authority. To assist us two concepts will help. Our locus of control and our locus of causality.

Locus of control

Locus of control (*locus* is Latin for place or location) refers to our fundamental belief about where the authority or power to execute our lives resides. It asks who has control. It can be any place on a continuum between external and internal locus of control. If we have external locus of control, we believe that some external force (person or situation) has the control. We believe we have the control if we have internal locus of control.

It is important to remember that this is a dynamic continuum and on this continuum is an important circle of influence. For example, you and I have no control over the weather. Whether it rains or not is totally outside our control, but we do choose what to wear when it rains. Our choice of gear falls inside our circle of influence. People with an external locus of control tend to complain that the rain prevents them from having a fun day. People with an internal locus of control have fun dancing in the rain.

"Some people feel the rain. Others just get wet." —Bob Marley

To illustrate the power of this concept I invite you to read *Man's Search for Meaning* by Victor Frankl. [15] He was a Jewish psychiatrist who survived the Nazi concentration camps. In his book he explains how they could predict who'd survive the day and who would not, based on their sense of agency. He also shares a personal story of how he could endure the whipping of the guards because he kept his locus of control internal. If it was possible for him to apply this mindset in those hellish circumstances, how much more possible is it not for us to do so in our day-to-day challenges?

Locus of control asks where things are controlled from. Locus of causality asks from where things are caused. It is also on an internal-external continuum. An internal locus of causality belief system basically says "I make things happen" and an external locus of causality belief system says "Things happen to me."

In thinking about these concepts I created a thinking tool I call the Autonomy Quadrants.[16] I combined the two concepts, locus of control and causality by placing them on two continuums as an x- and y-axis. This then forms four quadrants. Please note that in explaining the different quadrants I overgeneralize to emphasize a point. Real life involves a range of nuances.

The locus of control continuum is placed on the x-axis with the internal pole on the right and the external pole on the left. The locus of causality becomes the y-axis with the internal pole on the top and the external pole at the bottom.

Fig 4 – Autonomy quadrants

Quadrant 4 – External locus of control and causality

The victim quadrant. People who fall into this quadrant believe that some external power or person has control over what happens to them. They are powerless as things keep on happening to them. They have a strong victim mentality and tend to be stuck in the drama of this quadrant. It seems bad luck always follows them around. I notice that at some point they get addicted to the drama. So much so that they create the drama to experience the pity associated with it. Don't go there.

Quadrant 3 – External locus of control and internal locus of causality

The struggler falls into this quadrant. People in this quadrant have a sense of their own ability to make things happen, but they are always locked in a struggle against the powers that be. Because their locus of control is external (an external entity holds the authority) they tend to be easily influenced by the current situation. But they are always ready to act according to what they believe is important. People in this quadrant easily blame a named or unnamed external power (a secret society or autocratic authority) for some evil and then organize (initiate action) a rally against it.

Quadrant 2 – Internal locus of control and external locus of causality

In this quadrant we find the gambler. People who have a sense of control over their reactions, but because their causality is external, they live with a mentality that whatever hand of cards life deals them, they will make the best of it. They easily go with the flow of things and deal with whatever comes their way. This is a reactive way of living, and they need to learn how to take the initiative and make things happen for themselves.

Quadrant 1 – Internal locus of control and causality

I call people in this quadrant the creators. They have a sense of their authority to control their reactions and a belief in their ability to make things happen. They are the creators of their lives. I believe this is the healthiest quadrant and that we all need to grow this mentality.

To understand this model, it is important to know and accept that there is a definite circle of influence in the center of these four quadrants.

There are events that we have no control over, and which happen. For example, in 2011 an earthquake and tsunami hit Japan. There was no way the Japanese could control or cause this disaster. They were legitimate victims. But they quickly moved to the creator quadrant to rebuild what was destroyed. So should we when an accident happens to us. This model is dynamic, and we do not have to be stuck in one quadrant. Move. Activate your locus of control and causality from within (internal) as quickly as you can and create the reality that you want.

Remember the underlying assumption I shared in the introduction? That you have the ability to change your mind and choose your consequence. Well, here is the explanation for that assumption. By taking responsibility for your life, you become the creator of the outcomes you want, and you start to play seriously in the 40% of your potential.

Be warned as well. Taking responsibility for your life also holds in itself an uncomfortable truth. It leads you to lose a comforting illusion.

The truth is you have always been responsible for your life. The good and the bad. You created it. The ineffective belief that life as you have it now was given to you is an illusion. You created it. You have always been the creator; you have just not been aware of it. I am not referring to things that happened outside your circle of influence. A car accident for example (unless you were under the influence of alcohol or something). I am referring to the general state of your life.

It is uncomfortable when we realize that our external world is a reflection of our internal one. Yes, we are influenced by our conditioning, but not questioning that conditioning is choosing to accept it. Not consciously improving our conditioning, as this book argues we should do, does not change the fact. Your life is what it is because you choose it to be so, consciously or unconsciously.

Few people are willing to swallow this truth. But in this dark side of taking responsibility for the good, the bad and the ugly, lies a gift. While you created the life you have, you can also re-create it. And now that you are aware of better possibilities you can re-create an improved you. But you have to embrace the dark side first.

I remember an uncomfortable and bitter realization when I looked at myself in the mirror and had to accept that the chaos I was experiencing was my own doing. It took me days to get over it. But it was also a turning point in my life. It motivated me to be stronger at saying no to certain people that were not good for me. The decision liberated me to follow my dream assertively. Since then I have been living my dream, and experience flow more often than not.

So, yes, it is not *lekker* (nice), but it is worth it. Take the pill.

If

If you can keep your head when all about you
Are losing theirs and blaming it on you,
If you can trust yourself when all men doubt you,
But make allowance for their doubting too;
If you can wait and not be tired by waiting,
Or being lied about, don't deal in lies,
Or being hated, don't give way to hating,
And yet don't look too good, nor talk too wise:
If you can dream – and not make dreams your master,
If you can think – and not make thoughts your aim;
If you can meet with Triumph and Disaster
And treat those two impostors just the same;
If you can bear to hear the truth you've spoken
Twisted by knaves to make a trap for fools,
Or watch the things you gave your life to, broken,
And stoop and build 'em up with worn-out tools:
If you can make one heap of all your winnings
And risk it all on one turn of pitch-and-toss,
And lose, and start again at your beginnings
And never breathe a word about your loss;
If you can force your heart and nerve and sinew
To serve your turn long after they are gone,
And so hold on when there is nothing in you
Except the Will which says to them: "Hold on!"
If you can talk with crowds and keep your virtue,
Or walk with kings – nor lose the common touch,
If neither foes nor loving friends can hurt you,

If all men count with you, but none too much;
If you can fill the unforgiving minute
With sixty seconds' worth of distance run,
Yours is the Earth and everything that's in it,
And – which is more – you'll be a Man, my son!
Rudyard Kipling (1865 - 1936)

Blink 10

"The truth is everyone is going to hurt you. You just got to find the ones worth suffering for." —Bob Marley

In a word:

Belonging

The Tweet:

The universe is a whole. Everything is interconnected, and we are part of this whole. Something we seem to have forgotten.

The Post:

- As humans, we seek connection with other people.

- Most of us are in a state of disconnect.

- We search and take action to fit in, be part of, and be accepted and to belong.

- To experience a connection is to experience a sense of belonging.

- This need for belonging is fundamentally ingrained in our psyche and our survival instinct.

- Because our sense of belonging is so fundamental to our wellbeing, we cannot leave it to chance.

- We are all influenced by one another. We cannot not be influenced.

- Not all relationships are equal, more specifically, not all influences are equal.

- An important truth to realize is that we allow other people to influence us.

- We cannot control that they influence us; we control how they influence us.

- We manage this influence through active management of our interpersonal boundaries.

- Another tool to use in managing influence is understanding cognitive dissonance.

- Understand the dynamic interrelationship between your true self and your ego.

- Enter the monkeys — manage them well by using the ABC tool.

Sense of belonging

The universe is a whole. Everything is interconnected, and we are part of this whole. Something we seem to have forgotten.

The most obvious presentation of this interconnectedness can be seen in nature. Another example is how the World Wide Web mirrors interconnectivity. As humans, we mostly seek connection with other people. Although being connected is one of humanity's primary needs, most of us are in a state of disconnect. We do not feel connected to anything and are in a constant search to connect.

This is a sad state to be in because the reality is we are connected to everything. We are just not aware of it. It is a bit like experiencing gravity. We are constantly subjected to the pull of the earth's core, but not aware of it until we jump or fall. The same is true of our connectedness. The limitation of our senses and conditioning gives us the experience of being disconnected from nature, and from each other, and the unfortunate reality is that we experience this disconnect. Especially from each other, and this is what we have to deal with.

Therefore we search and take action to fit in, be part of, and be accepted and to belong.

But we are connected. We would not be able to exist without the connection to the whole that is our universe. This knowing that I am part of the bigger whole makes me feel safe. To experience a connection *is* to experience a sense of belonging. This need is so fundamentally ingrained in our psyche that I suspect it is encoded in our DNA. It is through this that we experience the connection we search for.

To belong is strongly connected with our survival instinct. A baby needs to belong and be connected to a caregiver. In prehistoric times our ancestors needed to belong and be accepted in the tribe. Banishment from a tribe equaled death as the saber-toothed tigers would easily kill a single human.

It makes sense then that we place such emphasis on belonging to a group of people, whether family, sports team, fan club or a nation. This primal drive to connect to other people plays itself out each time we meet someone. It is why the status quo is to be in a relationship with someone. It is why gangs are so strong in underprivileged communities, and why belonging to the golf club is so important in the affluent ones.

It also explains why being rejected hurts so much. Our primitive reaction interprets being rejected the same as the impending death of banishment from our tribe. The fear of rejection is strong in all of us and needs to be addressed specifically in our life journey.

Fear of rejection presents itself in a number of ways. Examples are the fear of public speaking, the hesitation to walk into a room of strangers, the compromises we make to keep the peace in our relationships. We strongly move away from people or situations where we anticipate rejection. And actively move toward people or situations where we perceive acceptance.

Understanding that the need for acceptance is so strong is the start of the process. This is one belief system that if left unexamined could wrap us up in a bunch of ineffective and limiting beliefs. We all need to re-educate this primitive conditioning. We are no longer living in prehistoric times. We do not die when we are rejected. Sure it hurts, but so does cutting your finger. The brain registers the same pain. I acknowledge some rejections are deeper than others. But we cannot give these experiences or anticipation of experiences the authority to dictate our happiness.

What we can do is to actively work on a constructive set of belief systems. Our sense of belonging is so fundamental to our wellbeing that we cannot leave it to chance.

Join me as we focus on building supportive and healthy connections with people. As research constantly shows, our happiness is influenced and largely determined by reciprocal relationships. So let us reframe our conditioning about other people and our connection to them. To do so, I would like us to explore the unequalness of relationships and the boundaries that go with them. I would also like to introduce you to the different phases that are present in all long-term relationships.

An important departure point is to acknowledge that we constantly influence one another. We might not be aware of this but we cannot avoid being influenced. It can be as simple as being aware of a man walking across the street, or we can be deeply moved by a child's laughter.

The biological building blocks that make this possible are called mirror neurons. Beautiful little things each that make it possible for us to pick up on other people's emotional vibes. These neurons enable us to be empathetic and connect with each other. We differ in how developed they are, but we all have them.

As with other talents, some of us are naturally gifted in using these neurons, but all of us can develop them. Many of us can run a 100 meters but Hussain Bolt, because of his remarkable talent and professional development of that talent (conditioning), can run it faster than most people on the planet. The point is we can all develop our mirror neurons. I will refer to mirror neurons again when we discuss emotional mastery.

We influence and are influenced. Yet not all influences are equal.

We can understand this cognitively. Our relationship we have with our boss is different from the one we have with our mother. We understand this intellectually, but we do not seem to remember it on an emotional level. We often allow people to influence us indiscriminately. Not all influences are equal.

The realization of this truth opens up to us to control the influence. I want to underline this point: We allow other people to influence us. To be more specific: We cannot control that they influence us; we can control how they influence us. For the uninformed, the influence plays out as their conditioning dictates and therefore can be easily manipulated. But we are the captain of our souls. We can decide and dictate the influence.

This is a powerful weapon with a double-edged blade. We can minimize the negative influence of people, but the same block of negative influence also blocks the reception of positive influence. A client had to learn to not allow his in-laws' criticisms to influence him. Unfortunately he also blocked out his wife's affection and adoration in the process. We need to be aware of this and manage it appropriately.

How? You may ask. The answer: Through the active management of our interpersonal boundaries.[17]

Boundaries

Boundaries are important in any relationship. Knowing your boundaries is simply being honest about what works for you and what does not. Another way of looking at boundaries has to do with knowing which influences are good for us and which are bad. Boundaries keep us safe. Knowing how boundaries work can assist in managing the influence people have on us. The skillful management of boundaries can also be transferred to activity and energy management.

There are different kinds of boundaries. Every person has them even though some are not strong. Boundaries can be likened to the process of creating privacy in your home.

Boundaries can be rigid. When you allow no one and nothing to influence you. You have built a wall around your house. Nobody can see in. This might keep you safe for now, but it also locks you in, and you have created your prison. It keeps you safe and lonely. Unfortunately, when you do need someone, no one can see that you need help.

Some boundaries are porous. There is a line in the sand, but anybody can move in and out. Your house has no curtains or doors. This type of boundary is unstable and inconsistent. People with porous boundaries sometimes allow something one day but not the next. We seldom know where we stand with them. People with porous boundaries tend to not like boundaries. They feel it restricts and suffocates them. That might be so from their viewpoint, but without personal boundaries you will not achieve much because you tend to not take responsibility for your actions. This is unsafe, and people with no healthy boundaries often overstep those of other people and leave them feeling violated. . A simple analogy. Consider a brick. In its most natural state is it nothing but a blob of clay. We can do nothing with it. But when we bake that blob of clay into a brick we create six-sided boundaries for the clay, and then we can build with it.

Healthy boundaries are flexible. Here your house has a fence with a gate. You have doors and curtains that can be closed or opened, depending on who is with you. People you choose to allow in can come in, but that same person can be asked to leave, and the door closed behind them.

Healthy flexible boundaries start with yourself and your personal ethics. Have you ever considered what is ethical for you? Have you taken the trouble to sit down and explore your governing value system? We all have a value system. It is conditioned into us at an early age. The question is: Have you evaluated these belief systems? Without a strong sense of internal value-driven thinking, boundaries will not work. Each of us needs to know what it is that we value above all else, and what we deeply respect. From this foundation, it is easy to say "No, this does not work for me" (aka, put up a boundary).

With strong, flexible boundaries we can manage the influence people have on us. To manage this it helps to know what the influence is. A positive influence may be someone who supports or mentors you. A negative influence might be someone who criticizes you or drains your energy for them to feel good. Sometimes one person can have both positive and negative influences. Take the time to label the influences the people in your life have on you. Once you have labeled them you can manage them. For example, you might have a boss that opens doors for you, but also criticizes you. Because you have labeled the influence, you can be grateful for all the opportunities and block the criticisms.

To take managing influences to the next level the following two tools will be useful. Let me tell you about monkeys and cognitive dissonance.

Cognitive dissonance

Cognitive dissonance is a term used in psychology to describe the discomfort felt when someone's personal beliefs and reality do not match. The major way in which we make sense of the world around us is by telling ourselves a story. We weave events and memories of the past together with explanations that are logical and that formulate a coherent and chronologically ordered story. This is a normal process of receiving information from events and people and placing this information in the logical place in our story line. In our story, we tend always to be the hero.[18] We experience cognitive dissonance when information comes into our system that does not align with our hero story. Like an alcoholic or gambler in denial. Nobody wants to be the bad guy, especially if one has a weak ego.

Allow me to pause a moment and explain the ego. We all have one. The ego has an important job to fulfill in our human interactions. It protects us. Its job is to keep us safe. It acts as insulation from the outside world. See your ego as the coat you put on when it's cold outside. It is your ego that protects you from walking down the street in your birthday suit.

It also surrounds your true self — the real you. All the beautiful, unique character traits and creative expressions that are in you. In our journey our task is to make our true selves come into their own. As a child it is easy. We are spontaneously ourselves. But then through conditioning, our ego forms protective layer upon layer around us in order to be socially acceptable (remember our need for belonging).

Some people grow a thick and well-developed insulation, and often this thick ego becomes the boss. That is when we have a disproportionate what-will-the-people-think mentality. The healthier space to be in is when the true self takes ownership of your life and keeps the ego insulation thin enough to do the least harm. This is emotional maturity. We cannot lose our ego. Our psyche will not allow us that. We need some form of the outer shell to protect us. But we can manage our ego more effectively. Hopefully this book will play a useful role in this process.

Back to cognitive dissonance and the process of dealing with uncomfortable information. When such information does come in, our ego automatically does a few things. Mostly it deletes it or throws away the information. In general people are not aware of things that do not make sense or fit into their paradigm. We call it willful blindness. The facts are there; we just don't see them.

When people do become aware of these facts, they use various defense mechanisms to protect their current story line. The most common is denying or projecting. Denying is easy. We dismiss the truth as a lie, or we dismiss the source of information as unreliable. Projection is when we accept the facts but assign them to someone or something else. Because we cannot incorporate an uncomfortable truth about ourselves, we give it to someone else. We say "It is your fault that I am unhappy" or "You made me do it."

Enter the monkeys.

Story to illustrate[19]

Two teenage girls living next to each other want to go to a party on a Friday night. They ask their dads if they may go.

The first girl's dad says "Yes, but you have to be back at midnight, or else you will be in big trouble." The second girl's dad also agrees and also gives the deadline of midnight, but adds that if she is not home on time, she is grounded the next few weekends.

Now, you know how things are with teenage girls and Friday night parties. They are having fun and midnight comes and midnight goes. And 1:00 a.m. comes, and 1:00 a.m. goes. At 1:15 a.m. they try to slip back into their homes.

As the first girl gets to the door, her father jerks it open and angrily says: "Where were you, you spoiled brat, is this the way you show respect for us. We work our asses off to give you a good home, and this is how you show your gratitude!" Then mom intervenes and says "Where were you, dear, we were so worried. We phoned the hospitals and police stations and morgues."

So dad sends her to her room with the words "You are in big trouble young lady, " and as she walks to her room, she thinks: 'Big trouble = Dad is angry + Mom is crying. No big deal, give it two or three days of making coffee and tea and all will be fine.' That night she sleeps like a log, but mom and dad are not sleeping because there is a monkey jumping around in their bed thinking: "Where have we gone wrong? Is there a future for our daughter? Will she become a drug addict?"

This is scenario one. Let's go to the neighbor's house and see how scenario two plays out.

The teenager also comes home 1:15 a.m. Everything is quiet at home. As she slips in, she sees mom and dad asleep on the couch. They had a movie, pizza and red wine evening.

As she tries to slip past them, the floor creaks below her feet. Dad picks up his head and says: "I am so glad to see you have chosen to spend the next few weekends with us."

That night mom and dad sleep like a log. The girl cannot sleep because there is a monkey jumping around on her bed. She had plans to see her boyfriend's big game next weekend.

Monkeys are consequences of choices and actions. We are all responsible for our monkeys. More specifically, we have primary responsibility for our thoughts, words, deeds, and emotions. As revealed earlier, consequences are the result of our belief systems, and we create our belief systems consciously or unconsciously. It is our responsibility to educate and train our monkeys through self-discipline and deliberately create belief systems that align with the values that our true self chooses.

What tends to happen is people do not want to take responsibility for their ugly dirty, smelly monkeys (cognitive dissonance). So they give them away (projection).

And here is the point of this long story. When we manage other people's influences on us, we do not need to take on their monkeys.

We have enough of our own and a hard enough time mastering them. We need to activate our boundaries to build strong and positive relationships with people. Through the deliberate management of our thoughts about how we connect with others, we proactively create our sense of belonging in a meaningful way.

For example, a friend may try and manipulate your guilt by saying "You made me unhappy." We now know this is not true. She (or he) is unhappy because her belief system interpreted whatever happened in such a way that it caused the emotion of unhappiness. Here are two major monkeys: her thought process and the resulting emotion. We do not need to own any one of them.

What we do need to take responsibility for is our process. The friend's comment 'You made me unhappy' is the activating event that enters our system (the influence). At this moment it exists as neutral sound waves our ears pick up. Our belief system filters these sound waves and attaches meaning to them based on our preconditioned interpretation framework. This is our monkey. We are responsible for this interpretation. We can accept it as it is or choose to change it. This interpretation creates a consequence for which we are responsible.

Let us say we feel guilty. We can now trace this feeling to a belief system that has something to do with our need for acceptance. We believe we are responsible for other people's good feelings so that they will like us and we can belong together. Our guilty feeling is the punishment to prevent us from doing it again.

This belief system has flaws, though. Firstly, we have taken our friend's feeling monkey (and sadness is not a fluffy cuddly monkey, but a sticky, stinky one) and by association also the belief system monkey. We basically say "I am responsible for creating the thinking pattern that results in my friend being sad." Secondly, behind this belief is a deeper belief system that goes something like this: "I am the general manager of the universe; therefore, I must control other people's interpretation framework that will result in them feeling good, and accepting me. If this does not happen, it will reflect badly on my universe management skills, so I will have to resign. What a shameful thing that will be."

Ridiculous, isn't it? Yet we all have a bit of this two-year-old mentality in us. Our ego loves the illusion of power and control that this immature mentality provides. It always keeps a bit of it hidden somewhere. I invite you to grow up and resign as general manager of the universe. Life will be so much easier.

What would a healthier reaction be to our friend's comment?

It starts with us taking responsibility for what is legitimately ours. We do this by drawing boundaries around the elements of this interaction (remember everything is only one thing) to contain what is yours and what is your friend's responsibility.

A typical but slowed down response could be: We start by acknowledging that our mirror neurons picked up on our friend's emotional framework. Therefore we can be empathetic to her experience.

Being empathetic is to acknowledge that her sadness is the result of her interpretation framework. It is important that we acknowledge this and not judge it as appropriate or legitimate. When we judge we immediately attach an interpretation to it. For now, we merely observe his process.

We see her feelings and interpretation as monkeys she is sending to us. I usually visualize myself playing tennis with the monkeys that come toward me. Some of the shots are so way out that I leave them. Some land in my court and I need to return them over the net. I do this by acknowledging my friend's process and the fact that she is projecting her monkeys onto me.

I then ask myself, "Is this person and the relationship with this person important enough for me to return the volley?" If she and our relationship are important, I engage further. If not, I just let it slide like water from a duck's back. Remember, not all relationships are equal. It is your prerogative to choose which are worthwhile to engage and bring inside your boundary and which you will contain outside the fence.

When I engage, I still do not take responsibility for my friend's monkeys. I engage by first acknowledging her feelings. "I can see you are sad", and then ask "Could you please explain how your interpretation of what I did caused your sadness?" (or something similar).

When I understand her interpretation and because I value our relationship, I will choose to change my behavior. My behavior is my monkey, and I can train it to improve our friendship.

I can also understand her interpretation and be of the opinion that her belief system is ineffective. I can then enter into a dialogue and mirror this ineffective interpretation framework. Through this process, we grow closer to each other. We become more connected, and our sense of belonging strengthens.

Okay. I know real life and real time relationships are not this clear cut. I am inviting you to think about your belief systems regarding your relationships and start to proactively manage them. Since nothing is permanent, we have a responsibility to make the important ones work well. We are the creators of the relationships that bring us happiness. Be involved in them because our meaningful and important connections need our attention and care to flower and blossom.

"The truth is everyone is going to hurt you. You just got to find the ones worth suffering for." —Bob Marley

Blink 11

"But let there be spaces in your togetherness and let the winds of the heavens dance between you. Love one another but make not a bond of love; let it rather be a moving sea between the shores of your souls."
—*Kahlil Gibran*

In a word:

Relationships

The Tweet:

Meaningful long-term relationships are the foundation stones of our happiness. This is anchored in our biology and grows us.

The Post:

- The important relationships tend to be our long-term relationships.

- Love has a biological foundation that anchors it solidly in reality.

- A committed long-term relationship is a surprising ally in our self-improvement.

- Understanding the different phases of such a relationship helps.

- Phase 1 –romantic

- Phase 2 –disillusioned

- Phase 3 –power struggle

- Phase 4 –friendship

- Our true identity consists of both the acceptable and the unacceptable parts of us.

Relationships

The important relationships tend to be our long-term engagements. Relationships that stand the test of time are those of love. I think you will agree with me that love is a popular theme in relationships. Regardless of whether it is a parent-child or a spouse connection, love is assumed to be the binding factor. I would like us to pause and become aware of our conditioning about love.

I lean on Harville Hendrix and Helen Fisher for my thinking. What I share here is my integration of their work. I recommend you read their work.

Helen Fischer studied the brain in love and came to interesting conclusions (Watch some of her YouTube videos[20]). The first insight I have taken from her work is that love has a biological foundation. This is important, as it anchors a normally perceived ethereal aspect of life solidly in reality. We love because our genes and hormones tell us to. Our conditioning dictates how we express and cultivate this natural aspect of being human. We cannot stop loving someone, but we can improve how we love them, so that is why we think about love.

Helen Fischer explains the different types of love as seen from a hormonal perspective. Beginning with the basic sex drive where testosterone plays the major role. Then the romantic attraction with dopamine, norepinephrine, and serotonin as the major players, and lastly attachment, with oxytocin and vasopressin as the stars in the show.

Fisher also asked why we love some people and not others. What she found is that our hormones lead us into relationships with a certain type of person. She identified four universal temperament profiles based on the predominant hormone present.

1. Explorers – predominantly have dopamine and norepinephrine in their system. These are part of the happy hormone family. Explorers seek excitement and fun and

things to do. They also are often reckless and non-reflective. Explorers link up with Explorers.

2. Builders – predominantly have serotonin in their system. This is the calm, relax and focus down hormone. Builders tend to be calm and controlled. Loyalty is important to them. They can also be stubborn or rigid. Builders seek other Builders.

3. Directors – predominantly have testosterone in their system. This is the conquering hormone. Directors tend to be competitive, emotionally contained and direct. Also impatient and uncompromising.

4. Negotiators – predominantly have estrogen and oxytocin in their system. These hormones are the relationship building hormones responsible for connecting and building trust. Negotiators tend to be imaginative and big picture people. Also tend to be naïve, indecisive and unforgiving. Directors and Negotiators attract each other.

I want to pause and emphasize an important point. We all have everything. Please do not box or label yourself or others by one dimension. When we do this, we limit our potential. We are beautiful multidimensional beings, and we should always remember this.

If these are the biological building blocks for our long-term relationships, we still need to know how to make them work for us. In reading this book you are in the process of examining your conditioning about relationships. Knowing how the 50% biological system works, gives us a good foundation. Then we need to understand the 10% conditioning about relationships as well.

Many aspects influence this conditioning. How the media portrays the ideal relationship. Selling us some product. This is easy to identify.

More difficult is the parental influence. We learn how relationships work as a child by observing our parents or adult caregivers. Unchecked, this conditioning repeats itself through generations. But we are in the process of reframing our conditioning to give our children an improved mental map, are we not?

Let's be honest. Most parents do their best. Parents, please give yourselves a break. Children give your parents a break. Most parents try their best with the knowledge they have at their disposal. Most of us succeed in more than one way. Inevitably we also make mistakes. The mistakes in this generation are the growth points for the next one. So lighten up and focus on what can be done now to improve tomorrow.

That said, let's get back to the process of improving our belief systems about relationships. I found that Harville Hendrix [21] helped me with a useful model so I would like to share my integration of his thinking.

Let us start at the beginning. As a child in the process of forming our personality we quickly learn what is acceptable to our caregivers and what is not. Taking into account that for our primitive conditioning acceptance is crucial for survival, children keep on modeling the acceptable behavior. This becomes our persona. The unacceptable behavior does not go away; it is also part of our unique self. It moves into the background. Our true identity, therefore, consists of both acceptable and unacceptable parts. On our journey to emotional wellbeing, one of the important truths to accept is that we are both light and shadow.

Remember, our egos do not want to accept the bad guy in the story, only the good guy. So people, driven by their egos, deny the self that is in the background. But this self is constantly asking for acceptance. As it is part of our being whole it continually knocks on the back door until we embrace it as part of us. I call these shadow selves our trolls. They are ugly, stinky, sweaty buggers, and like a naughty child they act out in the most inappropriate of times.

Carl Jung said "I'd rather be whole than good . . . wholeness is not achieved by cutting off a portion of one's being, but by integration of the contraries."

Yes, it is by embracing our trolls and by becoming friends with them that we become our true selves. En route to emotional maturity we all need to sit in this uncomfortable fire and converse with our trolls. We will be surprised to find that they have our wellbeing at heart all this time. That it is their intention to show us the way to our true power. We will find that in accepting our trolls we open the door to being more than what we can imagine.

Now I know this is not an easy process. I encourage you to engage in a proactive collaboration with a good therapist or life coach. It makes the difficult journey manageable. It is good to have someone reliable in your corner while you are slugging it out in the ring (arena).

THE MAN IN THE ARENA

Excerpt from the speech "Citizenship in A Republic" delivered at the Sorbonne, in Paris, France on 23 April 1910

It is not the critic who counts; not the man who points out how the strong man stumbles, or where the doer of deeds could have done them better. The credit belongs to the man who is actually in the arena, whose face is marred by dust and sweat and blood; who strives valiantly; who errs, who comes short again and again, because there is no effort without error and shortcoming; but who does actually strive to do the deeds; who knows great enthusiasms, the great devotions; who spends himself in a worthy cause; who at the best knows in the end the triumph of high achievement, and who at the worst, if he fails, at least fails while daring greatly, so that his place shall never be with those cold and timid souls who neither know victory nor defeat.

—Theodore Roosevelt

On our journey to create a better self, a committed long-term relationship is a surprising ally and a powerful tool. I think the primary purpose for such a relationship (like a marriage) [22] is self-improvement. To become our best selves. Is this not the biggest gift we can give our partner (and ourselves)? After all our true self is the reason they fell in love with us initially. So why do you think our relationships are such an important personal growth tool?

Allow me to try and explain by giving unsolicited advice.

Guys, we all know girls are beautiful to look at. Soft to touch and taste exquisite. But they are also full of crap. So when a guy decides to marry a girl, he should not marry her for her looks or sex appeal. These things change. The deciding factor should be: "Can I live with her crap?" (The same applies to a girl who wants to marry a guy. Just be warned girls, boys are bigger, and therefore they have more crap.)

If the guy decides, yes, he can live with her crap and marry her he will realize (if he is on this journey of self-enhancement) after a while that this crap is not his wife's but his own. He will then have a choice: a) Do I carry on unhappy with this crap under my nose or b) do I take this crap, turn it into manure and grow to my full self?

This process of using a long-term relationship as a personal growth tool makes more sense when we bring in Hendrix's four phases.

Phase 1 – the romantic phase:

In the romantic phase we are on a hormonal happiness trip. Remember Helen Fischer's work on the biology of love? So while our hormones intoxicate us, a psychological process plays out. Our shadow self, the one we hide in the background of our personality, joins us on this trip and feels great. At last, it also gets attention.

It is as if all our life we have been looking for someone to complete us. Let us liken this need for completeness to an empty square. Our shadow self, yearning for some nourishing attention, sees the person that triggers the hormonal intoxication as their savior. Notice the language we use when we are romantically in love: "You complete me" or "I feel whole when I am with you." We tend to say "Two halves make a full circle" and all those other clichés.

The truth is our hormones (dopamine, norepinephrine and serotonin) have zonked us, activated by the pheromones our noses pick up in the presence of the beloved. And like a drug addict we want to be in that person's presence all the time. We crave this high we technically give ourselves and go into withdrawal symptoms of moping and longing when we cannot have it (if the relationship breaks up). This tends to happen often in our adolescence when we are a ticking hormonal time bomb.

So let's say we go into this relationship longer than just a casual fling. We, at some time, then enter the second phase.

Phase 2 – the disillusioned phase:

After a while the hormones wash away as they tend to do. Picture a stream of water. If you throw dirt into the stream the water becomes muddy at first, but later clears itself up as the dirt is diluted and carried away. The same happens when hormones are dumped into our bloodstream.

In this phase we start to notice that our beloved is not who we thought they were. They pick their nose, or do not pick up their socks, etc. In phase 1 we saw our beloved as the perfect fit to our square. Now as our eyes become clear, we see them for the triangle that they are. Most relationships end here. We break up and go hunting for our next hormonal fix.

But if we made the commitment to a long-term relationship, we enter the third phase.

Phase 3 – the power struggle phase:

This is the most unpleasant phase of all. We hurt each other. Here you will find the screaming fights or cold wars. Most marriages end here.

What happens is that we want to change the triangle into a square and the triangle wants to change the square into a triangle. And nobody wants to be changed, so we resist big time. We long for the ideal world that our hormonal trip gave us because we believe the lie that our partner must make us happy. Our locus of control is external as we give our partners the responsibility to be everything to us. This is an unfair expectation which our partners cannot fulfill because they do not have the ability or the power. Only we have it.

We are all responsible for creating our happiness. When we realize this truth, we start to focus on changing ourselves. We can then move into phase 4.

I want to pause a moment and make an important aside. Every long-term relationship comes to a point where the partners need to make a decision: Are we going on or not? At this point in the journey, the ice underneath our feet is thin, and we need to proceed with caution.

I would like to point out two important things to remember at this point. The first is something my father-in-law taught me. He said, "Remember, it is inevitable that we will hurt each other in a relationship for we are but mere humans. But it is inexcusable that we humiliate each other." When you have been humiliated repeatedly in a relationship (physically or emotionally), walk away. You are entitled to be treated with respect. Respect yourself enough to walk out of such a dysfunctional relationship.

The second important thing. What in you creates these moments? You will come to this point again in any relationship. If you look back at all the relationships you have been in you will notice a pattern. Those you fall in love with tend to be the same type. The faces and places differ, but they repeat the same personality types. This is because we are attracted to those who mirror back to us the most important growth that needs to happen inside us. Remember I said that a long-term relationship is a personal growth tool? The majority of people will attract the same trigger until they have grown beyond it. So, consider this when you entertain a divorce or break-up. Are you willing to go through all this crap again with someone new or are you going to push through and break your barrier? I'll leave you to think about that one.

Phase 4 – the friendship phase:

In this phase as a couple we can become best friends. Friends accept each other with the shine and the shadow. We are not fair-weather friends that only take the sunshine, but true friends that walk in when everyone else walks out. We accept each other's light, and darkness.

In this phase, we allow each other the space to be, and create ourselves. We stand next to each other and become the witness to our partner's growth. We focus on changing ourselves. Giving room for our partner to grow and become the best triangle they can be while we work on being the best square we can be.

This journey is not as easy as I make it sound. It is messy and volatile as we lose limiting beliefs systems on our way to personal mastery. Nobody's ego raises the surrender flag without a good fight. So I recommend you and your partner go to one of Harville Hendrix's Imago Therapy retreats or any relationship growth events. Available worldwide.[23] This process is difficult enough, no need to re-invent the wheel. Ask for help.

Relationships with other people are the biggest and most influential factors in our happiness.[24] We cannot leave it to grow wild or be molded by societal or political correctness. We need to take responsibility and create sustainable healthy partnerships.

This then brings in the next important element in our human interaction. Our sense of justice and perceived status plays a unique role.

"But let there be spaces in your togetherness and let the winds of the heavens dance between you. Love one another but make not a bond of love; let it rather be a moving sea between the shores of your souls."
—Kahlil Gibran

Chapter 4

Status and Justice

Blink 12

"An insult can only be given where it is taken" —CJ Langenhoven

In a word:

Self-esteem

The Tweet:

We humans are herd animals that are influenced by the pecking order of our social community. We need to manage this in a healthy way.

The Post:

- Self-esteem: how we estimate ourselves.

- Social status: how we estimate ourselves in comparison to others.

- To function effectively we need to have a healthy estimation of ourselves.

- This estimation often happens in a social setting.

- When our self-esteem is demeaned, we experience an "away" movement.

- When our self-esteem is elevated, we experience a "toward" movement.

- Allowing people or situations to influence this movement creates a volatile situation.

• We humans are herd animals that are influenced by the hierarchy of our social community.

• In the up and down of the social pecking order, comparison to others is normal.

• We need to update our comparison software.

• In the new version, we compare ourselves to our former selves.

• You are enough unto yourself, and you can accept self as good and bad.

• When we meet someone, we evaluate whether or not we can be safe with this person.

• Based on this evaluation, we give the person permission to influence us, or not.

• When we upgrade our thinking software we manage this process effectively.

Self-esteem and social status

Self-esteem is simply how we estimate ourselves and often in relation to others.

For us to function effectively we need to have a healthy estimation of ourselves. We need to know where we come from, who we are, what we can do, and where we plan to go. This estimation often, especially in the beginning, happens in a social setting.

In our exploration of the "away" or "toward" movement it is understandable that when a person or situation demeans our self-esteem we want to move away from the person or situation. When a person or situation elevates our self-esteem we move toward that person or situation. This is natural and happens spontaneously.

The challenge with allowing people or situations to influence this movement is that these points of references open us to a volatile situation. If these external reference points are the only influences we allow, we will experience an unpleasant roller-coaster of high- and low self-esteem. This is not healthy. So let us create some stability by exploring our thinking about this aspect of our life.

The beautiful African spirituality Ubuntu gives a powerful description of what it means to be human. It shares: "I am because we are." We falsely assume we can survive on our own. The truth is, we are always connected or yearn to connect with other people, as we discussed in our sense of belonging. We flourish more in a community than outside one.

> *A student, who has an appointment, knocks on the door and the teacher asks, "Who's there?"*
>
> *The student responds, "It's me."*
>
> *The teacher calls out, "Go away."*
>
> *The puzzled student retreats, thinks and then returns to knock on the door.*
>
> *Once more the teacher asks, "Who's there?"*
>
> *This time the student responds, "It's us."*
>
> *"Come inside."*

Even so, it is important to understand that belonging to a community holds in itself a dynamic flux of influence and positioning to influence. One of these influences is the underestimated influence of social hierarchy.

I used to work with horses as co-facilitators in team development exercises. It is important when working with a herd to know the hierarchy in such a herd. You find the lead mare that takes care of the herd and just below her in the hierarchy there is a stallion to protect the herd. This hierarchy is in constant flux as the horses test each other to know who is where in the pecking order. This order literally dictates who eats when. When a group of people interacts with the herd, the horses mirror the human group, and the facilitators notice how the normal hierarchy changes as it says something about the interpersonal dynamics of the human group.

When we humans interact with each other, the same tends to happen. But unlike a herd of horses that stays fairly constant, the human community changes frequently. We often move into and out of different communities in any given time frame. We move from the family to the work community to friends or a sports community. In each one of these communities we tend to have different statuses or positions in the pecking order of the particular social hierarchy. In a professional community the hierarchy is formal and fairly obvious. You have the boss and managers and cleaner, etc. In a social community, the pecking order is not so clear and changes easily.

This positioning of ourselves in the social hierarchy is influenced by and influences our self-esteem. A big part of this is how we think and feel about ourselves in our social setting. Our social status is how we evaluate ourselves in comparison to other people.

Status can be formal and bound to a socially acceptable position, for example, you are the president a club. That is easy to deal with. Mostly it is the informal measurement between people that gives us trouble. It may happen that we feel inferior when we are in the presence of particular people. For example people with overactive egos that flash their success and achievements around. How do we deal with such an away movement?

Measuring ourselves

I would like to suggest that one way of dealing with this experience is to accept two normal and natural processes: First, it is natural to measure ourselves against others, and secondly, that allowing people to influence us is also normal. This is a natural process and needs some thinking about how to manage the effect on us in a more productive way.

There are people that advocate that we should not measure ourselves against other people. By doing so, they imply that we go against an all-natural phenomenon. My suggestion is that we accept that we instinctively measure ourselves and turn our focus to a more useful evaluation of the measurement tool we use. We can become more competent in measuring ourselves.

To do so, we first need to establish that we have the correct measuring instrument. It would be foolish to measure distance with a measuring cup. Distance gets measured in kilometers (or miles) and fluids in milliliters (or fluid ounces). We know how to use the correct measuring tool when we measure the world. The question is, what would the correct measurement tool be for evaluating ourselves?

Each one of us is genetically unique, each grew up in unique family structures and traditions, and each interprets the world uniquely. This immediately disqualifies other people (their lifestyle, tradition, social standing, etc.) as a fair measurement instrument. For how do we know what has happened in anybody else's life? Do we know the trials and tribulations someone has gone through to get to where they are? Can we see behind the social persona that everybody has to protect themselves? No, we can't. Nor can they know ours. It is biologically impossible as no two brains are alike. We only have our projected interpretations of what they choose to present at the moment we interact with them (Remember the "nothing is personal" ineffective belief system cuts both ways. Nothing anybody says or does is because of you).

What then would be a fair instrument to measure our social self-esteem? The only one that I can think of is our former selves. You know the one that achieved your previous success (or failure).

With this mindset we are right back into the observation of our conditioning and our choices. We can evaluate if our conditioning can be improved or if the choices we make can be wiser. Through this practice we can grow in self-confidence because we have an objective improvement as we get beyond our former self.

In the process of observing our former self (10% conditioning), we can keep in mind our uniqueness as well as our intrinsic value. Later we explore this in more detail. For now, it is sufficient to know we are enough. Not good enough; this immediately implies that you think in terms of an external comparison. Accept that you are enough. Sufficient unto yourself up to this point. Yes, you have growth potential. That is why we are busy with this book — to extend ourselves into the 40% of our potential.

To get there we are focusing on an alternative to the ineffective belief system of comparing yourself to others. To reframe this belief system into something effective we need to accept that we are simultaneously able and unable. We are competent in some things and incompetent in others. We have skills to do certain tasks but not others. We need to accept that up to this point in our life story we are a combination of wise and foolish choices, and that is the way we crumbled the cookie.

It adds no value to mope around about our past mistakes. But it does add value to learn from them. We need to stop trying to hold on to water that has flowed past, rather let the stream of experience move you forward. Also remember a mistake is always only identified in hindsight. No one deliberately makes a mistake. We take the information we have at any given moment and make the best choice we can. Taking the risk that the consequences of that choice will be good for us. Sometimes it is. Sometimes it is not. But we live with the consequence.

Knowing that we are enough, it is safe to assume that the same is true about those we meet. This equalizes the playing field. We are all trying to make this life we live worthwhile. As a young man, I once stood on the beach on a hot day. I had this intense longing to dive into the refreshingly cool water. At that time I was overweight so was conscious about my body image. I realized that there will always be someone with a better-looking body than mine (those guys that spend hours and hours sculpting their body in the gym) and there will always be someone that carries more excess weight than I do. I have the choice: Will I miss the cool refreshing water because I am comparing myself to an infinite continuum of variables? Or am I going to plunge in and enjoy myself? I did the latter and from that day on my life has been a ball. Any comparison is relative.

We are now aware of this thinking framework. When the automatic instinct to place yourself in a pecking order kicks in, you can now walk into a room full of people and evaluate yourself thinking, "Was I friendly to the doorman?" or "Did I smile warmly when I greeted, Jane?" All this is happening in the context of "Last week I forgot about the doorman, and he always greets me politely" or "In this week I noticed Jane's post on how she sometimes feels marginalized."

The second point to accept as natural is that we influence and are influenced. We discussed this when we explored our need to belong and will do it again when we discuss managing our emotion. At this point, our focus is on managing our social status, so we need to focus on the process of ascribed influence. When we meet someone, we instantaneously evaluate if we can be safe with this person and if we can trust them. Based on this instinctive evaluation, we give the person permission to influence us or not.

It is then also common to ascribe more to the person than we actually know about them. For example, if someone smiles when we meet them, we feel safe with them. If we allow our unexamined conditioning to run free, pervasiveness normally kicks in and we ascribe other positive attributes to the person based on our expectations.

But these expectations may not be based on facts. The person we ascribe with the positive attributes might be just the opposite. This is called the halo effect and explains why we love to meet celebrities and tell others about how we know them. We inaccurately believe that their goodness (goodness we ascribed to them in the first place) will rub off on us. This is also why celebrities get paid to endorse products. The halo effect rubs off on the product. So although this is a natural process, we need to learn how to be more accurate in how we use it. Remember, we are all human. We all eat, sleep and go to the bathroom. Manage this natural influencing process with more care and keep your esteem of others on par with your own (Do unto yourself what you would do to others).

In summary then, in the dynamic process of managing the "toward" and "away" movement of our self-esteem and social self, we now have an understanding of the instinctive hierarchical positioning our belief system puts us in. With this understanding we can reframe that belief system into an effectively calibrated measuring tool that measures us against our former selves. And as we measure others against themselves we can also start to manage their influence on us and ours on them.

The Invitation by Oriah
It doesn't interest me what you do for a living.
I want to know what you ache for
and if you dare to dream of meeting your heart's longing.
It doesn't interest me how old you are.
I want to know if you will risk looking like a fool
for love

for your dream
for the adventure of being alive.
It doesn't interest me what planets are squaring your moon...
I want to know if you have touched the centre of your own sorrow
if you have been opened by life's betrayals
or have become shrivelled and closed
from fear of further pain.
I want to know if you can sit with pain
mine or your own
without moving to hide it
or fade it
or fix it.
I want to know if you can be with joy
mine or your own
if you can dance with wildness
and let the ecstasy fill you to the tips of your fingers and toes
without cautioning us
to be careful
to be realistic
to remember the limitations of being human.
It doesn't interest me if the story you are telling me
is true.
I want to know if you can
disappoint another
to be true to yourself.
If you can bear the accusation of betrayal
and not betray your own soul.
If you can be faithless
and therefore trustworthy.
I want to know if you can see Beauty
even when it is not pretty
every day.

And if you can source your own life
from its presence.
I want to know if you can live with failure
yours and mine
and still stand at the edge of the lake
and shout to the silver of the full moon,
"Yes."
It doesn't interest me
to know where you live or how much money you have.
I want to know if you can get up
after the night of grief and despair
weary and bruised to the bone
and do what needs to be done
to feed the children.
It doesn't interest me who you know
or how you came to be here.
I want to know if you will stand
in the centre of the fire
with me
and not shrink back.
It doesn't interest me where or what or with whom
you have studied.
I want to know what sustains you
from the inside
when all else falls away.
I want to know if you can be alone
with yourself
and if you truly like the company you keep
in the empty moments.
By Oriah © Mountain Dreaming,
from the book The Invitation[25]

Blink 13

"Beyond our ideas of right-doing and wrong-doing, there is a field. I'll meet you there." —Rumi

In a word:

Justice

The Tweet:

The ethical and moral connections we all make around justice play a big role. These moral and ethical connections are deeply embedded in our cultural conditioning.

The Post:

- The sense of justice is the most complicated of the five movements.

- The movement is not difficult to understand. We move away from injustice or unfairness and toward justice or fairness.

- Find an anchor point in your thinking. A central departure point. Be honest about it.

- A departure point in the exploration of justice is human rights and various pairs of polarities.

- Each one of us has an evolutionary contribution to make. It is right that we are here.

- Be aware of legitimate vs imagined rights.

- One of the biggest culprits in experiences of injustice is unexamined expectations.

- An exact duplicate of the past experience leads to disappointment.

• The second danger of unexamined expectations is that we miss what is actually happening.

• A third alternative is to set conscious intentions and then let go of the outcome.

• Differentiate between "entitlement" and "privilege" and understand your thinking about them.

• Committing to the re-education of your sense of justice is difficult but worthwhile.

• Understand the four phases of moral development:

• Phase 1 - Black and White

• Phase 2 - Institutionalized

• Phase 3 - Relative

• Phase 4 - Commitment.

• Engage with the discipline of gratitude.

Sense of justice

The sense of justice is the most complicated of the five movements we have discussed up to now. Complicated because all of the previous movements, (social status, agency, the need for certainty and belonging) play a role in the sense of justice. The movement is not difficult to understand. We move away from injustice or unfairness and toward justice or fairness. It is the belief system we have about justice that complicates the movement and therefore needs the most thought.

Also important are the ethical and moral connections we all make around justice. And these moral and ethical connections are deeply embedded in our cultural conditioning. Cultural conditioning in itself is complicated and context specific. Our challenge to think about our thinking has just stepped up a notch.

Lately, my thinking about this concept has been stretched, and I would like to share my thoughts with you as a possible departure point to question your thinking about justice and fairness.

I believe it is a healthy thinking habit to be aware of and honest about the anchor principles or departure point of your argument. In this book it is the behavioral continuum I shared at the start of the book. I suspect we all do this but are not always aware of the belief system we departed from. Or if we are aware, we may not be honest enough with ourselves to see it as one out of thousands of possible departure points, or open enough to allow our departure point to be questioned for its validity. For the exploration of our thinking about justice, I suggest we take as a departure point the acceptance of our human rights as an anchor, and then explore various pairs of polarities.

In the world according to me, we all have a biological right to be here. We will not have been born if this were not so. Out of how many thousands of sperms, the one that co-created us got through to the egg, and we were conceived. And out of how many things that can go wrong during birth, for many of us ours was successful. Because of this miracle, I believe each one of us has an evolutionary contribution to make (some people would refer to this as fulfilling your destiny or following a calling). It is right that you and I are here. We have a right to be here.

Knowing you have the right to be here is just the first step. The United Nations has identified more than 30 universal human rights [26] that serve as an accepted departure point for the bigger society we live in. My question is how we manage our thinking about this.

My assumption is that our sense of justice originates in the understanding of our rights. When do we feel an injustice has been done? When we feel something we have a right to has been denied us. Is this not so? Unhappiness comes from our experience of being treated unfairly. As children, we assumed we had the right to an equal amount of cookies. When a brother or sister got more than we did, we felt it was unfair and usually complained about it.

Think about your recent experiences of being treated unfairly. It probably was in a context where you did not receive something that you expected to receive. Thinking about this, can you identify the expectation you had that it was fair that you receive it? Was that expectation based on a legitimate right or an imagined one? A legitimate right has an objective (mostly universal) principle behind it, the UN Human Rights Charter, for example. An imagined right is more subjective and often linked to our ego demanding certain privileges. In between these poles we find real life happening, where we need to manage (or educate) our expectations.

It might be helpful to distinguish between various concepts that play into our sense of justice. The ability to make finer distinctions in any situation is proof that we are looking intelligently at life. So let us do some exploring.

Expectations

Firstly I would like to explore our expectations. One of the biggest culprits in our unfounded experience of injustice is our unexamined expectations.

Expectations are informed by what we want based on past experience. We want the repeat of the past. There is nothing wrong with having an expectation. We should just be informed about what we are expecting. Usually, we expect to feel or experience something we know. It creates an anticipation of a good experience (toward movement) or bad experience (away from movement). There is a danger in unexamined expectations. Some people want the exact duplicate of the past experience, which cannot be as we already know everything changes. The disappointment based on the unrepeatable past often leads to an angry discontent.

"No man ever steps in the same river twice, for it's not the same river and he's not the same man."
—*Heraclitus*

A second danger lies hidden in unexamined expectations. That is, that the picture of how it should be, based on the past experience, is so strong that the person misses what is actually happening in front of him.

I have often found that the expectation is met, just presented in a different form. A person, attached to the past presentation often walks away unhappy because she/ he thinks they did not get what they wanted. They may have received more, just packaged differently.

For example, one of my clients expected to stay in the same room he liked at a hotel he frequently visited on his business trips. On one of his trips the manager showed him to a new room. The room was literally new. He was the first person to sleep in it. The room was a bit smaller than the one he was used to and liked. This bothered him because he liked space around him. He could faintly smell the paint and was on the verge of using it as an excuse to ask the manager to take him to his old room when the manager opened the curtains. The room had a huge window with a lovely view of the mountains. It benefits us when we observe and pay attention to what is happening right now and to suspend our preconceived ideas. Things just might turn out better.

There is a third alternative. That is to set conscious intentions for any situation. In this alternative, we take expectations to a new and more constructive level. Remember the five levels of focus discussed in Chapter 2? In this process we combine the first two levels — knowing what you want and planning how to get it. I listened to a motivational speaker a few years ago (cannot remember his name). He said: "Proper preparation prevents poor performance." The better you are prepared for any situation, the easier it becomes.

One of my cricket heroes, Jonty Rhodes, said: "You play like you practice." And this is true in most situations. Just be careful that all this preparation does not cloud your view of what is actually happening. Prepare as much as you can but when the moment arrives let go of all those thoughts and allow the moment to have a life of its own. This is important.

You have already resigned as general manager of the universe. Trust yourself and the process of living. What must happen, will happen. Only be present and pay attention. Open up space to be fascinated by what is happening before your eyes. Go into the flow and be surprised at what gifts come to you. Enjoy the moment.

"The more I practice, the luckier I get." —Gary Player

Entitlement and privilege

The second point of exploration in thinking about our sense of justice is the differentiation between "entitlement" and "privilege." It is important to state that not one of these terms is negative. They refer to legitimate elements in our world. We are entitled to certain things. We are privileged because we receive these things. It is the unweighted application (being on autopilot) of these concepts that makes life complex.

In my understanding, entitlement is the demand of favor or right to that which you do not have. Privilege already contains the favor or right, without necessarily doing something to get it. You are merely the recipient of the favor and not someone else. I think this is an important emphasis. Privilege is a favor that *you* have, and which someone else does not have.

There are people with an entitlement mentality or attitude that it is not pretty. In these cases, the demand is made for the favor without the necessary grounds to receive the favor other than that you want it or need it. I believe that this type of entitlement is rooted in a strong external locus of control. Such people, who feel they are entitled to something, usually demand it from some external person or power. They stand on the claim that they deserve something, seldom questioning the claim itself.

These two concepts, entitlement and privilege, have often had been stacked up against each other. There are people that feel they themselves are entitled to the favors that the privileged already have. The privileged tend to either feel guilty that they have favor and others do not, or they defend themselves against the anger of entitled-driven people.

For me, it comes down to your thinking about what you have and do not have. Every person is entitled to clean drinking water, for example. Once you have clean drinking water, you are privileged because there are people that do not have it. We can say you are entitled to certain rights and once you have them, then you become privileged because you have them. That said, we also need to acknowledge that there are layers to this complexity.

In our society education is a basic human right. Something that everyone is entitled to but does not have equal access to. Those that do have access to it are privileged. But not all education is of the same standard. Now we put down another layer. Those who have a basic education are privileged in comparison to those that do not have an education. Are they then entitled to quality education of a high standard? Those privileged to have access to this higher standard of education. Do they see it as a privilege or do they simply accept that it must be so?

The challenge of growing up with privilege is that you do not always realize that you are privileged. Privileged people often fail to understand the anger of the people fighting for the favor they already have. And in this we become polarized. The have-nots believe they are entitled to the same favors that the haves assume to be normal. The egos of the haves tend to resist this drive for equal favor, for then the privilege is removed as everybody will have the favor. Mainly because, paradoxically, in a conversation about privilege, ego tends to come from a place of scarcity. The egos of the haves then want to keep the feeling of being special (privileged) because of the instinctive hierarchy (discussed in the awareness of our social status section).

There is nothing wrong with these natural movements. It becomes problematic when we become attached to one side of this dance and then perceive unfair treatment when our expectations are not met. This attachment to "not having" something is surprisingly common. Please remember that attachment in our argument is the emotional weight we place on a singular outcome. I am surprised (and saddened) by the strength of this attachment as people allow the "not having something" to become part of their identity.

This need not be so. I find people who attach to only entitlement become strugglers as explained in our argument on agency and autonomy. They tend to become revolutionist in the story they tell about themselves and often fail to grow beyond the limiting one-dimensional identity.

As humans we are more than just one thing. We are beautifully multidimensional (I will probably repeat this a few times). So I would like to invite you to explore an alternative. How would it be if you committed yourself to the re-education of your sense of justice? The commitment being the dedication to a greater cause, regardless of the series of outcomes.

Our innate sense of justice fuels our conscience and personal ethics. Most people take the teaching of what is right and wrong over from whoever is teaching them, without question. Again this is acceptable in a child. But an adult has the responsibility to re-educate her- or himself.

I understand that this is easier said than done. In this re-education it might be helpful to know about the four phases of moral development. I would like to share my simple understanding of this. [27] The four phases come from Roman times where the military officers were taught how to obey orders. Through the ages it has been refined and adapted. It helped me to understand that there are phases we go through and that these phases are relevant to various concepts regarding fairness and justice.

Phase 1: the black-and-white phase. This is a simple dualistic way of thinking. There is one right way, and it is the way I believe it to be. I am right, and you are wrong. This way of thinking often ends in conflict and can become the cause of rigid behavioral choices.

Phase 2: the institutionalized phase. People came to understand that there are gray areas between black and white. They also realized that the rigidity of behavior was counterproductive. But they still believed in the right version of the truth. Therefore they came together and agreed on what the truth was. It becomes a collective agreement that rules (belief systems of what is right or wrong) and governs society. Should you want to be part of this society, you need to adhere to these rules. If not, you are excluded.

Phase 3: everything is relative. All roads lead to the top of the mountain. There are multiple truths. As the poet Rumi says "There are hundreds of ways to kneel and kiss the ground." This develops from the earlier phase as individuals realize that the different collective agreements are much the same at their core. The differences that do exist are easily played down as minor differences. What you believe is right for you is right for you. What I believe is right for me is right for me. This phase opens up space for all belief systems to coexist next to each other as long as the individual belief system is not affected.

Phase 4: I call the commitment phase. This is where the individual comes to a moral space in which conscious choices are made at a personal level regarding what is right and wrong. It differs from the relative phase in regards to the acknowledgment that not all belief systems are good for the collective. In this, they align with Phase 2 in that there is a collective right and wrong, but differ from that phase in the sense that the collective right and wrong includes more than one specific group.

In a sense it goes back to the first phase because someone in this developmental phase consciously chooses non-negotiable truths. It differs from the first phase in that they acknowledge that there are alternatives to this truth and simultaneously can defend their choice of their version of the truth. In this choice they are open to being convinced otherwise, but the change will only come through solid and thorough arguments as their truths tend to be lived, experienced and debated first hand.

Icons like Mahatma Gandhi, Nelson Mandela and Mother Theresa embody this phase. Although flawed according to their own standards, they knew what was right for them to do and by doing so, they changed the world.

Gratitude as an alternative

I would like to invite readers to engage with the discipline of gratitude when re-educating their thinking about justice. Being grateful for what you have is an age-old mental discipline that few people practice even though it has a scientifically [28] proven powerful effect on our happiness.

"If the only prayer you say in your life is 'thank you' that would suffice."
—Meister Eckhart

Being grateful for what you have is a healthy alternative for the often experienced shame or anger that those in privileged positions experience. It is also a good exercise for those who are on the entitled spectrum of the continuum. It is easy when you do not have something to fixate on what is lacking or absent. But we also know now that we have a choice as to where to focus our attention. We can choose which wolf to feed. We can shift our locus of control internally and focus on that which is already present in abundance. The discipline of gratitude creates a mentality of abundance and opens us up to see more.

This does not mean we must accept social injustices and just be grateful for what we have. No, we still need to address the inequality or unfairness. Just think, how would it be different if the unfairness were addressed through abundance rather than from a place of scarcity?

So, what are you grateful for? This question can be misjudged as something your grandmother asks, but it has power in it. Asking the question has the power to shift your focus from what you do not have to what you do have. It is a support question working in the background of all our thinking. It supports the mindset of abundance and lays the foundation for our defenses against negativity. We will receive many a curved ball on our journey to fulfillment. When we are still untrained in our mental resilience, an exercise in gratitude will help us bounce back faster.

Please do not underestimate this practice of being grateful. Remember our default error detection mode? Well this mode, if unchecked, can pull us down into a spiral of negativity. We do not get what we want, and that creates emotions of anger and fear as we observe the "not getting" in the light of the ever-present uncertainty. We easily succumb to an it-will-never-happen pit of despair.

We counter this with gratitude for small things. Warm clothes, a house, legs to walk on, and a mind to think with. Owning a car or knowing a friend with a car. Being grateful for what you have is like watering a plant. It grows. You will find that you get more of what you have as you bounce back into pursuing your goals.

That said, the biggest personal challenge most people will have to face is the maturity to be grateful for the challenging aspects in life. I once walked my feet into blisters hiking down the coast. It happened on the first day of an 11-day hike. My friend and I had been planning this trip for a year, and then this happened.

I knew about the principle of gratefulness but never practiced it. So I tried it out as we could not turn back. I must confess I struggled with being grateful for the blisters. I had to go as so far as to say out loud "Thank you for the blisters" with every painful step.

It turned out that because of the blisters I was forced to walk slowly and so had the time to notice the intricate artwork of nature that would have gone unnoticed had I walked at my normal hiking speed. Today, other people are amazed at the beauty I see around us — a crystal drop of rain on a leaf of grass or a golden eagle nesting in a high building. And because of this, I see more in people as well, and this feeds into my coaching.

So try it. Be grateful for the bad and the ugly and see how you can incorporate their power over you and center it in yourself. Gratitude is a powerful tool. Use it to change your world.

One day, a father of a very wealthy family took his son on a trip to the country with the firm purpose of showing his son how poor people live. They spent a couple of days and nights on the farm of what would be considered a poor family. On their return the father asked his son, "How was the trip?"

"It was great, Dad."

"Did you see how poor people live?"

"Oh yeah."

"So, tell me what you have learned from the trip?" asked the father.

The son answered, "I saw that we have one dog and they had four. We have a pool that reaches to the middle of our garden, and they have a creek that has no end. We have imported lanterns in our garden, and they have the stars at night. Our patio reaches to the front yard, and they have the whole horizon. We have a small piece of land to live on, and they have fields that go beyond our sight. We have servants who serve us, but they serve others. We buy our food, but they grow theirs. We have walls around our property to protect us; they have friends to protect them."

The boy's father was speechless.

Then his son added, "Thanks, Dad, for showing me how poor we are.[29]

The process of re-educating our belief systems around fairness and the clarification of our entitled rights and privileges is a complex and sometimes difficult road. It is crucial though that we pay our bill by thinking through this as it fuels our emotional reactions. This will be seen in the next chapter. I trust that the thoughts about these structures become a viable departure point as we re-educate ourselves.

We need to continuously work on the subtle away and toward movement as our belief systems dictate. We need to re-engage again and again as we become aware of how we reactively act out of the autopilot zone of our conditioning. As my sister taught me in our long dialogues on the back roads, seconding for her husband and eldest son's Fish river canoe race, some conversations never end.

"Beyond our ideas of right-doing and wrong-doing, there is a field. I'll meet you there." —Rumi

Chapter 5

Emotional Consequences

Blink 14

"Knowing others is intelligence; knowing yourself is true wisdom.
Mastering others is strength; mastering yourself is true power."
—Lao-Tzu (604BC)

In a word:
Emotions
The Tweet:
I think emotions are the most important part of being human.
The Post:

- You cannot control emotions; you need to manage them.

- The biological foundations of our emotions are hormonal energy.

- To better regulate them, we need to understand the emotional reaction process.

- The amygdala and other centers in the brain play an important part in this process.

- Distinguish between dwelling on and sitting with emotions.

- We have emotions for a reason. They have survival functions.

- The survival function of love is growth.

• If you understand that fear wants to protect you, it becomes your friend.

• Anger's function is to protect us from injustice.

• Sorrow's function is to heal from loss.

• Self-mastery is the aim of emotional regulation.

• It is a life-long journey of creating harmony between our heart and our mind.

• Managing emotions is also an important stepping stone in creating flow in your life.

• Flow refers to "optimal human performance" or "the zone" in which we function.

• Flow is the result of a challenge complementing our abilities.

• We need challenges to live a meaningful life.

Emotions

I think emotions are the most important element of being human. Yet, despite the popularity of concepts like emotional or social Intelligence, few people have mastered their emotions.

The average person, often on autopilot, seems to either reject, downplay or is enslaved by his/her emotions. Others belittle emotions as a primitive form of being human and advocate being only rational. I find this perspective lazy and limiting. We are first emotional, then rational beings. Our emotions are deeply embedded in our biological behavior and cannot be denied.

In thinking about our thinking, emotions are the consequence in our ABC model. There can be other consequences, I know. But these are the consequences that hit closest to home. It is the first awareness we have that something is happening even if we can seldom put a name to it. Emotional consequences activate a powerful force in our lives for good or evil, yet they tend to be left unexamined. Because of their importance to our wellbeing, it is crucial we make a conscious effort to effectively manage these consequences.

I see emotions as a beautiful stallion. If left wild, it will run all over the place and might hurt you if you try to ride it. But if you build a relationship with the stallion, win its trust and train it, you will be able to ride it. It will take you further than you would have gone on your own.

Please note that I say train the stallion. I did not say break it in. Some people break in their horses. This is a cruel process, leaving the horse traumatized. Horse trainers, who train their horses, make loyal friends for the rest of their lives. Most people think they have to control their emotions or break them in. You cannot control emotions; you need to manage or regulate them.

Emotions are nothing but hormones in our blood stream. Once there, you can do nothing to get them out of your system. Remember Helen Fischer's insight around love, that it has solid biological foundations? The same is true for other emotions. The emotion we experience and label as love or fear or sadness is a unique cocktail of hormones that our limbic system dumps into our bloodstream. Different hormones activate the cells in our bodies in different ways [30] to generate different types of energy. For example, adrenalin injects our cells with excess energy to jump us over a wall if we are terrified.

Since the biological foundations of our emotions are hormonal energy, we can focus away from simply being emotional and focus on the managing of this activated energy. A simple equation is: Emotion

= hormones = energy. We know energy cannot be destroyed, though it can be translated into another form. Mastering our emotions then involves the difficult process of channeling the energy created in a constructive way.

Before we go into how to better regulate our emotions we need to have a better understanding of how the reaction process works. To achieve this better understanding we need to further explore how the brain works.

The brain consists of numerous areas that deal with various functions. [31] For example, the area responsible for seeing is at the back of the head and the language center on the left side. For our purposes, we could divide the brain into three areas: the reptilian brain (brainstem and cerebellum), the old brain (the limbic system) and the new brain (neocortex).

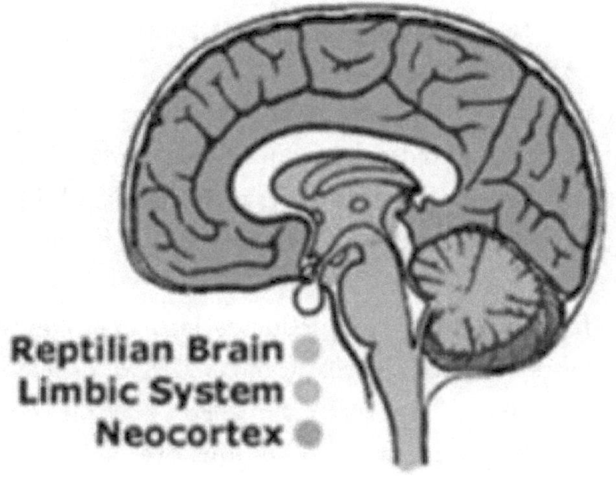

Fig 5 – The evolution-designed brain

Of course, the brain is a complex organ, beyond my simplistic explanation of its functions. This explanation is an attempt to communicate a complex process in an understandable way. For our purpose and conversation, we need to grasp that each of these three areas is responsible for a wide array of functions. For example, the reptilian brain is responsible for the most basic functions needed for survival: breathing, heartbeat, digestive system, etc. The old brain is responsible for the next level of survival, big muscle movements, hormonal regulation and so forth. The new brain is responsible for the higher functions of survival which include analytical and creative thinking.

Amygdala

In the old brain there are several centers, one of which is the amygdala. The amygdala is basically the security center of our brain. I liken it to an old sheriff in the old wild Western movies. With an office full of wanted posters.

So let's say you see a snake. The image of the snake is faxed to Sheriff Amygdala by the occipital lobe responsible for decoding light signals received from the eyes. Please note the old technology. The old brain (some call it the blind brain) is wrapped up in a primitive state of mind and is not in touch with reality. It depends heavily on the other regions of the brain for its information.

Sheriff Amygdala looks at his wall of wanted posters and sees one of them is of a snake. Through the ages man has learned that snakes are dangerous so he pulls the lever to tell the rest of the limbic system to react. The limbic system dumps adrenalin into the bloodstream, which activates your muscles. You jump and land five meters away. Meanwhile, the signal arrives at the neocortex, which analyzes the situation. We now see it is a rubber snake that one of the neighborhood boys was playing with. We breathe deeply and relax.

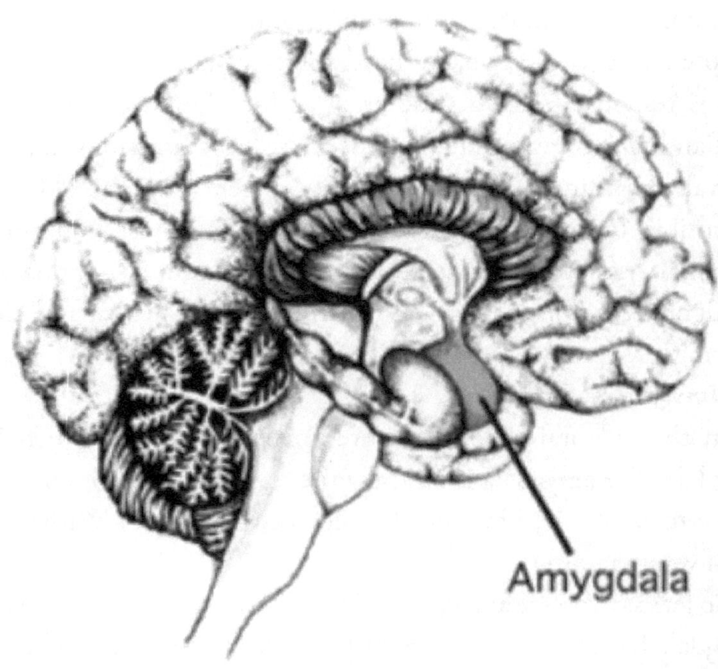

Fig 6 - The amygdala

This process happens much faster than I can explain, but you get the idea. For the sake of survival, we need this reaction to be instantaneous. When a lion wanders into the room, you and I cannot waste time debating whether this lion is a vegetarian or not. We run. Luckily for us lions seldom wander around anymore. But our sheriff has not adapted to the times and all those wanted posters have not been updated. Those posters represent our deep-seated belief systems about our safety, and many are in serious need of review. The creators of those belief systems, the conditioners of our mind (our parents, society and instinctual beliefs), though not necessarily knowledgeable, employed creative imagination while conditioning our minds.

The process of emotional regulation is the process of updating our wanted posters (re-educating our deep-seated belief systems). This regulation process starts with labeling the emotion. It is important to label correctly. Many clients struggle with labeling their emotions and therefore cannot regulate them effectively.

Labeling feelings

In this chapter, I hope to share a framework so that you can label feelings more easily. Please note a few important distinctions. First, I distinguish between feelings, the experience of the emotion, and emotions, the biological state we are in. Most of us are aware only of the feeling, and some struggle to name it. To understand that feelings have an emotional foundation that can be regulated through conscious training makes things easier. Second, in the process of emotional regulation, it is important to label and not dwell on feelings. Labeling acknowledges they are there. We can now manage them. Dwelling on them is an over-concern with the emotional experience. It's like fueling a fire. Some people build emotional bonfires, and this destroys them and the relationships around them.

A short sidetrack. There is an important difference between dwelling on your emotions and sitting with them. Dwelling on them is not healthy. People become their slaves. They build this huge emotional fire of being unhappy so that the unhappiness consumes them. At some point, their identity becomes "I am unhappy" rather than just "I have the emotional consequence of being unhappy." The consequence then becomes the boss rather than the true self experiencing the result of a process.

When we sit with our emotions, we do a brave thing. Not always enjoyable especially when they are negative. This is when you step into the fire and allow it to purify you. It is the process of reaching out to the trolls that present themselves, and befriending them. Not a pleasant experience but a deeply enriching process. This is the way to master ourselves. When we sit with our emotions we listen to their message.

We come to learn the unique sound of their voice, and we come to understand the weird way in which they look after our wellbeing. To come to this point we need to know them better, so let us explore this.

Have you ever wondered why we have emotions? Each of our emotions has a survival function otherwise they would not have evolved with us. I suggest we explore these functions to re-educate our belief systems.

When thinking about this it helps me to think in terms of various emotional families. For example, we could be slightly irritated with someone or furious with them. Both emotions are part of the anger family; they differ in intensity. In my world, the four principal emotional families are Love, Fear, Anger and Sorrow. [32] Of these four, Love and Fear are the two primary families with the biggest influence. There are other smaller families like Hope or Shame, but we will only focus on the big four. We begin by asking ourselves about the survival function of each of these. Do yourself a favor and explore the survival function of the other smaller emotional families.

Love

Love is probably the easiest. I label this survival function the growth function. Thinking about it in the most primitive form, love is about procreation; it is our genes' way of ensuring their future, making sure that the line continues. On a less primitive level, when we love something or someone we want the best for it or them. We want our child to grow up and be healthy and happy. We want our favorite sports team to win the championship.

Love's function is improvement, being better off, growth. When we do a good job at work, love fuels it. When an entrepreneur follows his or her passion and grows their business, it is a work of love. Love to me is more a verb than a noun. Remember the hormonal energy needs to be used. I therefore define love as whatever you do (or do not do) to leave the person (or thing) you love better off (improved). We can explore this definition later, but first I think we need to look at something interesting about love.

Building on the insights we received from Helen Fischer, I would like to introduce you to an old part of the mammalian nervous system called the periaqueductal gray (PAG), way down in the center of the brain. Now the PAG is a busy organ, but simply put its main two jobs are to protect us from pain by connecting us socially, and turning us on so we reproduce.

Here are two insights I invite you to think about. First, notice the position of the PAG. Deep down near to the foundations of our evolutionary development. For me, this is significant because it explains how love can conquer fear. The PAG and amygdala work together but is seems that the PAG can override the amygdala when a mother faces death to protect her baby. The second insight is that our biological love is nestled in the 50% behavior governed by our genes. This says something about the capacity available to us (50% + 40%) if we can recalibrate our conditioning (10%) about love.

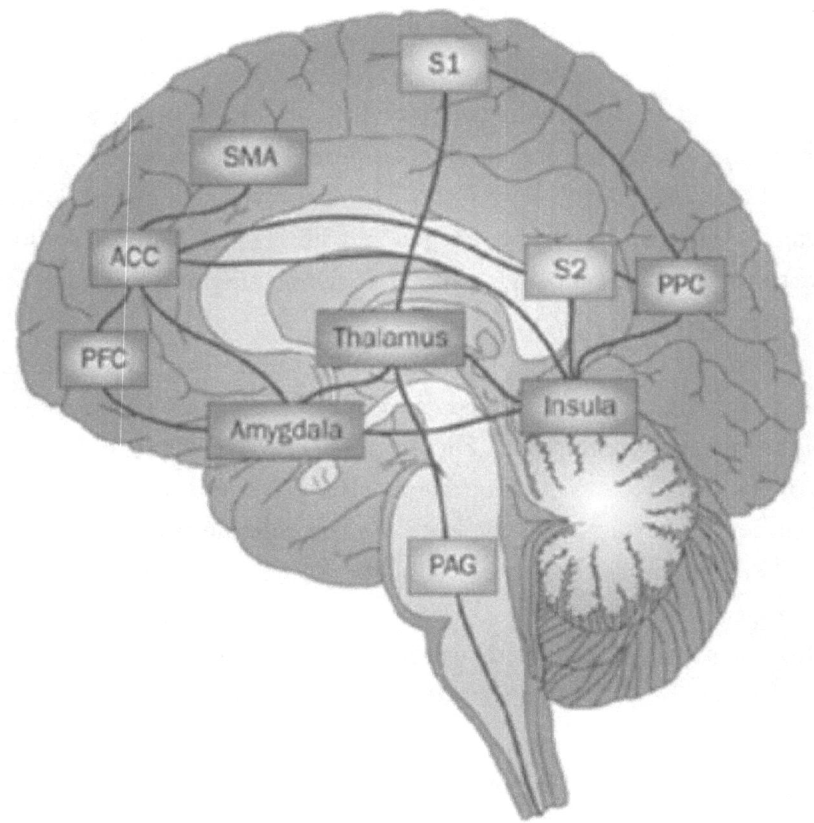

Fig 7 - Periaqueductal gray

These two insights confirm how deep seated our sense of belonging is. It also leads to a deeper understanding and positioning of the power of our compassion. When we observe someone else's pain, the same brain area is activated as if we feel pain ourselves. It seems that our mirror neurons are one of the biological building blocks enabling us to empathize with others; our brains are intensively wired to do so. The question then is not if we have the capability to empathize, but what do we do with this capability?

More specifically, let's explore our conditioning around this capacity to love. For it is there that we let the wires short circuit the most. It has become popular to think that the human species is but a selfish one. This is so, but it is only a half truth. The other half is that we are also a collaborative species. We have evolved the way we have because we have learned to work together.

Working together asks that we love each other. Knowing this, I invite readers to explore their belief systems about the themes associated with love. Themes such as forgiveness, altruism, and kindness. There are many books written around these themes, so I will not be able to add that many new insights. But I would like to pause a moment around kindness.

If you want to travel fast, travel alone. If you want to travel far, travel together —African Proverb

At my father's funeral, my nephew read a beautiful poem he had written. One of the lines stood out because it captured the essence of who my father was: *"In a hard world he was brave enough to be soft."*

My experience of how kind my father was is vividly engraved in my memory. I remember a butterfly that flew into the house, struggling to get through the window pane to freedom. My father cradled the butterfly in his big hand, muddy from working in the garden, and released it outside.

To me, this is a kindness. Helping another to move from struggle to a better future. Being kind to one another is the practical exhibition of love. What you do or not do to leave the one you love better off. Kindness is the act of benevolence that leads to a better future. Start with being kind to yourself. Build it out to those close to you then to strangers. And here is the challenge. Be kind regardless of the fear, whether it is fear of rejection or loss of status. Be brave enough to be kind in a hard world.

"I learned that courage was not the absence of fear, but the triumph over it. The brave man is not he who does not feel afraid, but he who conquers that fear." —Nelson Mandela

Fear

Fear is a misunderstood emotion. There is a multitude of voices going around saying, "Do not be afraid," "Fear is keeping you back," or "Fear is crippling you." This creates the expectation that fear is a negative emotion. So much so that some people are afraid of fear.

At the same time there are heaps of people suffering from anxiety, too much stress and struggle to function well in their context because they are afraid. Fear is not something that can be wished away. It is important that we examine it properly.

I think fear is your friend. Yes, fear can also be your foe. It can hold you back and prevent you from living your life to the fullest. But if you understand that all fear wants to do is protect you, it becomes your friend. Fear's evolutionary function is to warn us if there is a threat to our safety. For example, when you notice a slight discomfort when you speak to a stranger, pay attention. Fear is sending you a message. Unfortunately, the message gets lost in translation as our survival instincts kick in. It will add value if we sit with our friend fear, and ask: "What is the specific threat in this situation?"

Let me explain the process. When our Sheriff Amygdala receives the fax he activates the limbic system to protect us. Most of the blood (oxygen) moves to that part of the brain to ensure survival. Our brain lid flips open as the neocortex is depleted of blood and oxygen. We are in survival mode, and that is why we act irrationally. When we ask our amygdala "What is the threat?" it cannot answer, so it sends blood back to the neocortex to answer the question. The lid closes again, and we regain control. Always ask questions. Those who ask the question hold the power. Remember this.

Even when you have a full-blown anxiety attack, you can ask your fear "What is the threat?" Be kind to yourself when you do this. Remember, your system is flooded with adrenalin. Your old brain cannot give you an answer immediately. Be patient. Work with a therapist, use medication if necessary to help protect your brain.

On this point, please remember, medication is not the final answer. Rewiring your belief system is. Medication is merely helpful to rewire thinking. Medication will not solve your problems. You will have to do the hard work of reprogramming yourself.

Medication is also not the enemy. There are people that think taking medication is unnecessary. The truth is sometimes our brain needs help. Like when your body is depleted of its strength after running a marathon. You have to restore its strength by resting, eating and drinking. Your brain needs the same attention.

But unlike your body that does not need to run every hour of every day, your brain is always on. It never switches off, and sometimes it happens that it runs out of fuel. Yes, a part of your brain rests when we are asleep. That is why sleeping well is part of our basic health routine. But sometimes, especially when there are periods of stress or major changes, it will do no harm to protect your brain with medication. Like when you take vitamin C when you want to prevent a cold.

When we ask our friend fear what the threat is we are using our ABC tool in reverse. The Consequence is the emotion of fear. By asking the question, "What is the threat?" we explore the Belief System. Please notice the wording of the question. We do not ask "Why is there a threat?" This question puts us at the problem level of attentional focus, and our belief system will automatically churn out a variety of reasons. This quickly places our locus of control externally. We then give the power to the threat.

When we ask "What is the threat?" we keep the locus of control internal because we are only observing our environment. When we observe the threat as a neutral Activating Event we keep the power within ourselves. We open up space to examine our belief system about the event and act constructively.

We need to distinguish between imagined threats and real threats. Real threats do not need to be analyzed. If there is a lion in the room, run. Trust your instinct and act. But real threats are rare. It is not every day that your house is burning. But every day, when we deal with people and society in a social context, there are imagined threats hidden around every corner. These we need to re-examine, and educate and update the wanted posters in our sheriff's office.

In summary then, when we master our emotional regulation in regard to our friend fear, we need to update our software regarding what we perceive as a threat.

Anger

Let us move on to anger. What do you think is the survival function of anger?

I think anger has been discriminated against. It is a unique emotion that also wants to protect us. But where fear protects us from threat, anger protects us from injustice. And as seen in the last chapter, justice is a complicated matter. Anger is also complicated. It is the one emotion that receives the worst press. Probably because it is most commonly presented negatively and destructively.

What most people do not realize is that all emotions have a negative element. A dark side. Too much love, for example, smothers the one we love — a mother who does everything for her child because she loves him/her, also inhibits the child's ability to solve problems. The negative side of fear is that it freezes us into inaction.

The negative side of anger is destruction or violence. It is this destructive element that most of us resist. We move away from anger because we instinctively perceive that the violence will cause rejection and we know the strength of wanting to belong. But anger does not need to destruct. Anger also has a positive side. Whereas the negative side is destruction; the positive side is constructive and creative.

We become angry when we interpret an event as unfair. Unfair because we have a belief system that we have a right to some specific outcome. But now there is an obstacle, someone or some situation that blocks us from receiving or attaining this outcome.

Here again, we have to distinguish between an imagined unfairness that is nestled in our ego and real unfairness that is based on a principle or chosen value. Also remember there are degrees of anger. We can be slightly irritated or furious. All of them are part of the anger family and therefore important to label correctly. But regardless of the label, or whether it is imagined or real, we still need to deal with the energy in our system by managing or regulating our anger energy.

How do we do it? We can simply ask the question: "What is unfair about this?" Weigh the perceived unfairness as real or imagined and choose the channel for the energy. We can then choose to either destroy or create with this energy. If we choose to be destructive, we simply break through the obstacle. We build a bridge over the obstacle when we choose to be constructive or creative.

Building a bridge takes longer, I know, but it also gives us the opportunity to save a relationship. Anger in its purist form is richly seamed with love. Most people miss this. Especially men. Unfortunately, men in this world have predominantly had just the negative example of anger to mimic. Few of us have a picture of what a constructive flow of anger looks like. That said, I believe constructive anger is the gift men have to offer this world.

We are the builders of this world (yes, I know this could be interpreted as gender stereotyping and that women also have anger and can be creative, but I think there many men than need to hear this). When we build a business to succeed, it is the anger energy that is being channeled in a constructive way. When we create something — a product or a piece of art or, especially, when we build a relationship — we are using anger energy.

The point is we have a choice in which direction to channel the energy: constructive or destructive. We all need to sit with this troll and listen carefully until we understand the message of love or fear behind the anger. I think anger is constructive when it is laced with love and destructive when it is laced with unexamined fear. Anger understood, can be a unique gift to the world. *"Anger is the deepest form of compassion, for another, for the world, for the self, for life, for the body, for family and for ideals, all vulnerable and all, possibly about to be hurt. Stripped of physical imprisonment and violent reactions, anger is the purest form of care,"* says David Whyte[33].

One last point. Remember anger (as with all emotions) is energy in your system. You have to use it. If you bottle it up, it will either implode or explode. Both of them are destructive. Imploding is anger against yourself. This is presented in the form of depression or self-sabotage. Exploding is when you break the wall or someone's nose. Use the energy constructively by voicing your experience of unfairness. Say no. Draw the boundary. If you cannot do so immediately, go for a jog or walk. Translate the energy into something that can be a legacy of which you can be proud.

Sorrow

The last big emotional family. Sorrow. Sorrow or mourning is also one of those emotions people try to evade. But as with anger and fear, this emotion's primary function is to serve our wellbeing. Specifically, sorrow's function is to help us heal from loss.

Most people associate loss with life-shattering events such as losing a loved one or losing an arm or leg. These are the obvious and painful traumas that we go through. But each one of us goes through mini losses every day. Every expectation not met is a loss. Whether we are late for an important appointment or we are kept waiting is an expectation not met. Not getting the position at work or making the sports team, going through a divorce or breakup are other examples of the daily losses we face, all at different levels of intensity. Regardless of the intensity, we go through the mourning process as described earlier is one of the skills we need to master in dealing with change.

Sorrow's energy is not always as spectacular as those of the other emotions. It is more of a quiet, subtle energy. And mostly it takes time. Remember your heart is broken. Just as a broken leg needs time to heal, so does your heart. The average time it takes to mourn the loss of a loved one is 2–5 years. That said, also remember everybody mourns in their own way so I share this as a generalized time frame.

You have to judge when your process is complete. (Please consider professional help if you go through a serious loss or trauma.) I am not saying you should sit around and mope for two years if you did not get the job. Mourning needs to be appropriate to the intensity of the loss. As with the other emotions, our ego creates imaginary losses, and we need to learn how to get over ourselves. Getting over myself (ego) is one of the great liberating experiences in my life. It shed the heavy attachments to unrealistic expectations and freed me up to see the world in a new, simpler and more joyful way.

Rule number 6: Don't take yourself so seriously. No one is getting out of life alive.

When mourning (for big or small losses), do not fight back the tears. Tears are an appropriate release of energy. Cry your heart out. It is the healing balm your broken heart needs. I would just suggest you do it in a safe place, on your own or with a trusted friend. When my clients trusted me enough to cry in my presence, I always stood in awe. I felt like taking my shoes off as this was holy ground I had the privilege of standing on. Also give yourself more time to do things. When you normally write a report in a day, give yourself two or three days. Take time just to sit and do nothing. Open up space to heal.

We have to heal on our own. Yes, there can be support from friends and family, but healing from loss is one fire that purifies us in the most intense ways. At best, friends and family are the witnesses of our inner journey, but we have to walk the road alone. Good news. Those who have gone through this fire and made it are legion. We are cheering you on in the grandstands next to the road. You will make it and be the richer because of it, regardless of the scar.

Most Beautiful Heart[34]

One day a young man was standing in the middle of the town proclaiming that he had the most beautiful heart in the whole valley. A large crowd gathered and they all admired his heart for it was perfect. There was not a mark or a flaw in it. Yes, they all agreed it truly was the most beautiful heart they had ever seen. The young man was very proud and boasted more loudly about his beautiful heart.

Suddenly, an old man appeared at the front of the crowd and said, "Why, your heart is not nearly as beautiful as mine."

The crowd and the young man looked at the old man's heart. It was beating strongly, but full of scars, it had places where pieces had been removed and other pieces put in, but they didn't fit quite right, and there were several jagged edges. In some places, there were deep gouges where whole pieces were missing.

The people stared — how can he say his heart is more beautiful, they thought?

The young man looked at the old man's heart and saw its state and laughed. "You must be joking," he said. "Compare your heart with mine, mine is perfect, and yours is a mess of scars and tears."

"Yes," said the old man, "Yours is perfect looking, but I would never trade with you.

You see, every scar represents a person to whom I have given my love – I tear out a piece of my heart and give it to them, and often they give me a piece of their heart which fits into the empty place in my heart, but because the pieces aren't exact, I have some rough edges, which I cherish, because they remind me of the love we shared. "Sometimes I have given pieces of my heart away, and the other person hasn't returned a piece of his heart to me. These are the empty gouges — giving love is taking a chance. Although these gouges are painful, they stay open, reminding me of the love I have for these people too, and I hope someday they may return and fill the space I have waiting. So now do you see what true beauty is?"

The young man stood silently with tears running down his cheeks. He walked up to the old man, reached into his perfect young and beautiful heart, and ripped a piece out. He offered it to the old man with trembling hands.

The old man took his offering, placed it in his heart and then took a piece from his old scarred heart and placed it in the wound in the young man's heart. It fitted, but not perfectly, as there were some jagged edges.

The young man looked at his heart, not perfect anymore but more beautiful than ever since love from the old man's heart flowed into his.

They embraced and walked away side by side.

~ The End~

Starting to thrive

So why would we engage in managing our emotions?

I think it is a crucial step in opening up the door to thriving through self-mastery and creating flow.

Self-mastery is a life-long journey of creating harmony between our heart and our mind. It is also the one common element successful people own. They work on themselves. I hope that by reading this book you will have gained useful perspectives and tools to assist you on your way.

Knowing your emotions intimately is also important in dealing with other people. Remember our mirror neurons (Chapter 2) when we discussed our sense of belonging. Our mirror neurons pick up the emotions of others. The unintelligent and unconscious person will assume that this emotion I feel is mine. Knowing your emotions enables you to distinguish between someone else's emotion and your own.

Take for example the scenario when someone comes into your office and shouts angrily at you. Your immediate reaction would be to feel angry at the person. But if you know your emotions, you can ask yourself: "Is this my anger or just this person's anger my mirror neurons have picked up?" We know mirror neurons are the gateway to interpersonal influence.

So we have a choice. We can allow the other person's anger to influence us and dictate our reaction, or we can be proactive and turn the situation around by influencing the person with our calm energy. In this way we manage the flow of energy and become masters of ourselves.

Managing your emotions is also an important stepping stone in creating flow in your life. Flow refers to "optimal human performance" made popular by Mihaly Csikszentmihalyi. He focused his work on that seemingly elusive zone when we are joyfully totally consumed by an activity. His work demystified this zone and made it accessible to all who are willing to do the work. A definition of flow is:

> An altered state of consciousness in which the mind functions at its peak, time may seem distorted, and a sense of happiness prevails. In such a state the individual feels truly alive and fully attentive to what is being done. This state is distinguished from strained attention, in which the person forces himself to perform a task in which he has little interest. [35]

There are nine elements present when flow is generated:

1. There are clear goals every step of the way.

2. There is immediate feedback to one's actions.

3. There is a balance between challenges and skills.

4. Action and awareness are merged.

5. Distractions are excluded from consciousness.

6. There is no concern about failure.

7. Self-consciousness disappears.

8. The sense of time becomes distorted.

9. The activity becomes "autotelic" (an end in itself, done for its own sake).

I suggest you read Csikszentmihalyi's book to understand the concept better.

For our conversation, I would like to share a useful tool I picked up while I lectured in Sports Psychology.[36] It breaks our approach to the life of flow into four quadrants. The X-axis is our perceived ability, competence or talent. The Y-axis is the perceived degree of challenge or difficulty we face:

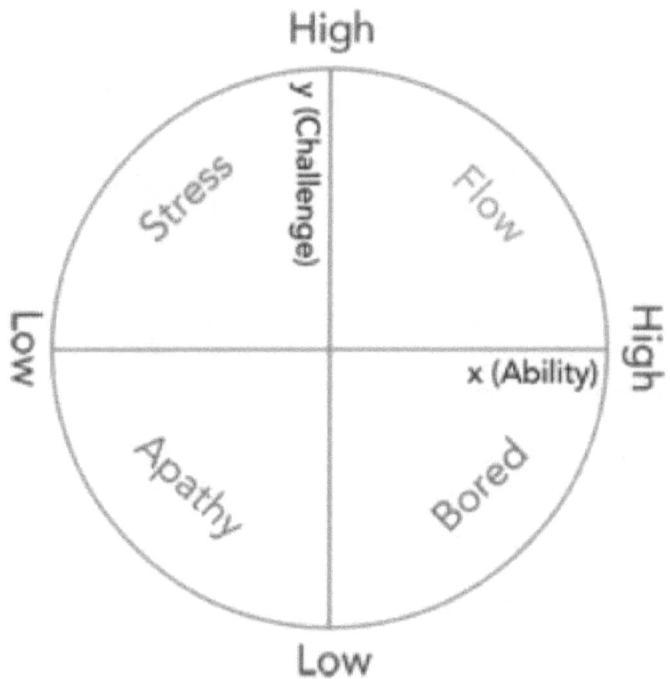

Fig 8 - Flow Quadrants

If the ability is low and the challenge is low, we are in an apathy zone. We have no motivation to do anything.

If the ability is high and the challenge is low, we tend to be bored. "This is easy," we say to ourselves and our mind drifts.

When the perceived challenge is higher than the perceived ability, we go into the stress zone.

But when the level of challenge compliments the level of ability, we enter into flow: the optimal performance zone.

So how do we use this tool? When we feel stressed, we can either adjust our assumptions (belief systems) about the challenge, make it smaller or less difficult by breaking it up into manageable pieces. Or we can adjust our assumptions (belief systems) about the level of our ability. Remember previous successes, or transpose a specific skill that we are competent in to this situation.

Another important point to take from this is that we need challenges. As the poet Browning says "Ah, but a man's reach should exceed his grasp, or what's a heaven for?" The assumption that in life for me to be happy everything must be easy is an ineffective belief system that originates in an inflated ego. To function optimally, to be joyous, we all need to engage in something meaningful. We ascribe meaning to something when we have given ourselves to it. We tend to underestimate the value of those things that we get easily. In contrast, we place a high value on things we have worked hard for, when we camped outside our comfort zone to gain our desired vision.

So if you want to perform optimally and be in your zone then accept the challenges. Every one accepted will ask you to pay something, whether it is time, energy or money. It need not be a struggle, but it will ask effort. Nothing happens until you commit to this. Once you commit to living life in flow, you will find things align to propel you in this way. Goethe understood this: "Concerning all acts of initiative (and creation), there is one elementary truth, the ignorance of which kills countless ideas and splendid plans: that the moment one definitely commits oneself, then Providence moves too."

In conclusion, remember emotions are the herbs and spices of life. They give depth and aroma to our experiences. But as with creating a delicious meal, too much of one spice kills the taste. You and I, in the journey to regulate our emotional consequences, need to learn when to add what herb and what spice. We do this by accurately labeling our emotions, adjusting our belief systems and intelligently observing the activating events coming from our environment.

The next chapter will explore the observation of our world in more detail.

Knowing others is intelligence; knowing yourself is true wisdom.
Mastering others is strength; mastering yourself is true power.
—Lao-Tzu (604BC)

Chapter 6

Observing the World

Blink 15

"Our eyes are shattered glass windows. Therefore we need to learn how to look sharply" —Koos du Plessis

In a word:

Observing

The Tweet:

With the randomness of how reality collapses into our experience of it, the best thing we can do is to learn how to look skillfully at life.

The Post:

- Become aware of your own Meta thinking.

- We can look at life in three different ways: Analytically, Creatively and Systemically.

- Analytical thinking takes your thinking apart to understand it better.

- Creative thinking puts things together to create a new something.

- Systemic thinking sees the interrelationships between elements.

- Learn how to see beyond the obvious.

- There is a difference between the name of the thing and what goes on.

- The magic of creative thinking lies in being fascinated with the world.

As you may have noticed the chapters are following our ABC thinking tool described in Chapter 1. We started with B, our belief systems; we then moved over to C, our emotional consequences. In this chapter, we want to take a look at the A: activating events

"Look at" is where the emphasis falls. With the randomness of how reality collapses into our experience of it, the best thing we can do is to learn how to look skillfully at life. An ability that, when mastered, can serve us well. When I was growing up there was a songwriter [37] who wrote these words which, translated into English, would go like this: "Our eyes are shattered glass windows. Therefore we need to learn how to look sharply." In this chapter I hope to open something up for you about the way you look at the world.

I am aware that this is another way of exploring your belief systems, but for me it is on a different level. Let's call it a meta level. My invitation to you is to become aware of your meta thinking through the various aspects I present here. According to my world view when we become conscious about our thinking, we can look at life in three different ways: Analytically, Creatively and Systemically.

There are volumes written on each one of these themes, so what I share here is not the definitive work on them, rather a shot at a simple introduction. And hopefully, it will encourage you to read more about them.

A simple placement on the differences between these types of thinking is that analytical thinking takes what you are thinking about apart to understand it better. Creative thinking puts things together to create a new something. I would like to begin with and focus on systemic thinking which involves seeing the interrelationships between elements.

Systems thinking

Systems thinking is not something new. Peter Senge introduced it to the business world in the 1990s, and before that it was already in use in various sciences. Today it is used in a variety of fields. These fields give the word meaning appropriate to their context. For our discussion, I would like to coin the way of thinking as systemic, at the risk of stating the obvious.

When we think systemically, the first thing to know is that we are part of various systems. We cannot avoid it. The road system, telephone system, electricity system, economic system, our family system and so forth.

It helps to think in terms of subsystems. Within our body are examples of subsystems. Respiratory, digestive, neurological, and so on. Each of these subsystems is built up of various subsystems and those subsystems have their subsystems. We can go on until we break the subsystems down to an atomic level.

But we can also go bigger. Our body is part of a subsystem in our family, our family is a subsystem in a community, the community in our country, our country in the continent and the world and we can go on up to the universe. The picture in my head is that of one of those Russian Matryoshki dolls that stack inside each other.

Fig 9 - Matryoshki dolls

Why does it help to think in terms of subsystems? Knowing that everything fits into everything else can overwhelm us. How do we know when something begins or ends? By identifying a subsystem, we draw a boundary. Within this boundary (even if it is a temporary or imagined one) we can observe the interaction with other subsystems. Observing the interrelatedness between subsystems touches the core of systemic thinking.

We touched on interrelatedness when we discussed our need for belonging in Chapter 2. This is a more technical look at the same thing. To understand interrelatedness, we need to understand the different types of systems and their unique inputs and outputs. A closed system is simple enough but rare. It does not have an input or output. An open system has an input and an output, and there are various types of open systems. Most healthy systems also have a feedback loop. The interactive and collaborative nature of healthy systems needs feedback to sustain the correct flow of output and allow sufficient input.

For us, once we have identified the subsystem and noticed the input, output and feedback loop between subsystems, we can start looking for patterns. The two basic types of patterns are a balancing pattern and a growth (reinforcing) one.

A simple and practical example is eating. The food we eat is the input into our body and its subsystems. Healthy eating habits keep our body in balance. There is feedback from our body to say when it needs new input (hunger) and when it has had enough. Eating unhealthily and not listening to the feedback results in gaining weight (growth).

The balancing pattern is one that strives to achieve the unique condition of homeostasis. Remember our need for consistency. All systems want to keep the status quo for as long as possible. But at the same time, all systems need to grow. So we have this field of tension between these two patterns.

Knowing that these elements must be present in subsystems, we can expect one or the other pattern when we observe a system. We can also expect the other to present itself at any time. A simple analogy is interest on money in the bank. Should you save an amount in the bank, interest is added, and your money grows. Or should you use your credit card, interest is added, so your debt grows (not all growth is good). To manage your debt, you pay a monthly amount. This is an external input into the credit card subsystem, and the growth is reversed to move back to the balance of zero debt. On the savings amount, an external input might be inflation (which is part of a different subsystem), and the value of your money might also be zero after a few years unless you keep on adding an amount to sustain the growth.

The tension between balance and growth is constant.

My invitation to you is first to learn how to see patterns.[38]

I suggest you start with the following mindset: Remember that everything is just one thing. If something happens, it will probably only happen once. If it happens a second time, you can expect it to happen a third time. If not, then it was a fluke. But if it happens then a pattern can start to form, and you can expect the same behavior to happen again.

Patterns, routines, habits are all elements of our drive for consistency. Try and become aware of your own patterns or habits. Are they serving you well? What is the belief system driving this behavior? Can you improve this belief system so that your patterns can serve you better? Do you notice behavioral patterns in your relationships? Do these patterns serve both parties in the relationship? Do you see patterns in your client's behavior? How can you use this to grow your business? The question is "Is it working for us?" If not, what new input do you need to allow in a subsystem to create the best outcome?

Learn how to see beyond the obvious. Our eyes tend to stop looking at the most obvious and first object available. For example, we see the car driving by, but not always the person in the car. When hunting, hunters need to learn to see beyond the branches of a bush. The deer is hiding in the undergrowth, and the hunter needs to look beyond the first layer of leaves and branches.

In life, we also need to learn how to look more deeply. Do not always accept the first answer presented. Wait to form your opinion about someone until the next time you meet that person. People present only a segment of themselves in the short time they interact with us. We do the same. They normally present what they want you to know at that time, but there is much more to a person than that one presentation. We know this to be true about ourselves as well. Look beyond the leaves; see the real prize hidden away. Wait for a pattern to emerge. Form your opinion and make your decisions based on a pattern not a once-off incident.

Analytical thinking

When discussing analytical thinking we need to distinguish it from critical thinking. Critical thinking is the process of questioning everything in order to determine the right or wrong of something. You question the source, the messenger, the motivation, the timing, the context, everything. In itself this is an appropriate skill to have in some circumstances, but not as a default mode of thinking. When I think about critical thinking I ask the question "Right and wrong according to whom?" This in itself is a critical thinking question, I know. I have found few thinkers that are competent enough in this thinking skill to be purely critical without the value judgment of some right or wrong model.

Most of us have a moral value system that colors our critical thinking. In itself, there is nothing wrong with this, as long as we are honest and conscious about this value system. Few people are.

Analytical thinking is the process of taking things apart in order to understand them better. We use it to break down a series of complex bits of information. It uses different points of view to achieve a better understanding of the internal cause and effect of what you are studying. Analytical thinking uses facts to support your conclusion and train of thought. If the facts do not support your conclusion, you change your conclusion, not the facts. When you have a complex problem or solution to find, you will use your analytical skills. You would use the five W questions: What happened? When, how long for? Where did it happen? Who made it happen? Whom did it happen to?

The object of analytical thinking is a deeper understanding not just for the sake of understanding, but to be better positioned to use the object of your observation (or not if it is not appropriate). Again we have to learn how to look beyond the obvious.

I once stood in a national park in front of a tree. I was in awe. I needed to sit down and lean back onto my elbows to see the top of the tree. Spectacular. And in front of the tree was a copper sign stating "This tree is 300 years old." Duh. I could see that. But in life, we often use copper signs. We try to capture something vast in simple words in order to carry it with us. All language has this function. Words represent shared meaning, enabling us to communicate.

But it also limits us to a few symbols that try and represent something greater than the symbol. Analytical thinking is the process of looking beyond the copper sign. It moves us beyond the sign and compels us to touch the tree, smell it, taste its bark and wonder how deep the roots go and what type of ground can keep such a tree anchored. Please do not stop thinking at the sign.

> *"This boy said to me, 'See that bird standing on the stump there? What's the name of it?' I said, 'I haven't got the slightest idea.' He said, 'It's a brown-throated thrush. Your father doesn't teach you much about science.'*
>
> *I smiled to myself because my father had already taught me that [the name] doesn't tell me anything about the bird. He taught me 'See that bird? It's a brown-throated thrush, but in Germany, it's called a halsenflugel, and in Chinese, they call it a chung ling, and even if you know all those names for it, you still know nothing about the bird — you only know something about people; what they call that bird. Now that thrush sings, and teaches its young to fly, and flies so many miles away during the summer across the country, and nobody knows how it finds its way,' and so forth. There is a difference between the name of the thing and what goes on." —Richard Feynman*

Creative thinking

There tends to be a preconceived idea that creativity only belongs to the artist. That one has to create an artwork to be creative. This assumption then stops with an object of art, like a painting or song. This is a false assumption. To think creatively has to do with creating.

Creative thinking links directly with our belief system that we can be creators of our reality. Remember the four autonomy quadrants in Chapter 2? We know the foundation of creative thinking is the belief that we have control over our reactions and that we can take the initiative to make things happen. It is anchored directly in the inherent belief of our authority to live intentionally. Creative thinking is putting all this together.

The magic of creative thinking originates in being fascinated with the world. Creativity links directly with our ability to learn. As children we learned to walk, talk and know our way around the world by trying things out and seeing what happened. We all smile when we see the wide-eyed amazement of children when they explore their world. And that, in essence, is creativity, the exploration of what will happen if ...

"One prerequisite for originality is clearly that a person shall not be inclined to impose his preconceptions on the fact as he sees it. Rather, he must be able to learn something new, even if this means that the ideas and notions that are comfortable or dear to him may be overturned."
—David Bohm

What will happen if we add this to that? What will happen if we stop doing something unhealthy? What will happen if I listen to understand my partner, regardless of my opinion? Creativity is embedded in every aspect of our lives, and it asks us to go beyond our conditioning. We are creative when we upgrade our belief systems and this is scary. Our need for stability will kick in big time when we explore alternatives. And our egos will speak up loudly about our social status.

But creative thinking asks us to move beyond what we know into the field of the unknown. It asks us to lose our fear of being wrong. My clients have often answered my questions with "I do not know." Now, this was usually a cop out because they were either too lazy to think, or not used to thinking in a focused way about their dilemma. But to me, this is such an exciting answer for it implies that we can find out. That we can play in the creative field of potentiality. Creative thinking loves not knowing. Some call this beginner's mind.

Not knowing is but the first step. The second step is to pay attention. See what is really in front of you. We discussed this earlier.

Press pause on drawing conclusions. Wait to see if there is something else. Be interested and fascinated. Be inquisitive enough to experiment and be prepared to be joyfully surprised. Every time we make a new connection or find out how things can be renewed, our brain rewards us with a dopamine injection. This happy hormone rewards us with a lovely freedom, a lightness that allows us to move forward with confidence.

"The truth of a life really has little to do with its quality. The quality of life is in proportion, always, to the capacity for delight. The capacity for delight is the gift of paying attention." —Julia Cameron

Be forewarned. As mentioned earlier, this comes with a responsibility: The responsibility to create the life we choose. It is of no use if we just go on a happy trip without capturing the energy into something concrete. This creative process asks to be rewarded with the completed product whether it is a cake, a successful business, or a healthy relationship. You cannot play in the field of potentiality and not leave the world a better place. So please pay your dues.

"There is vitality, a life force, energy, a quickening, that is translated through you into action, and because there is only one of you in all time, this expression is unique. And if you block it, it will never exist through any other medium and will be lost." —Martha Graham"

Chapter 7

Conclusion

Blink 16

"Finally, brothers and sisters, whatever is true, whatever is noble, whatever is right, whatever is pure, whatever is lovely, whatever is admirable—if anything is excellent or praiseworthy—think about such things." —St Paul

In a word:

Process

The Tweet:

Who you are is what you do. Thoughts, feelings, words are just intangible elements of the process. What you do crystallizes everything into reality.

The Post:

- Ask the important and age old question: "Who am I?"
- A vital answer is: "I am in process."
- We are in the process of dying, while in the process is living.
- So pay attention to what is done. And to what is not done.
- Not doing is as important as doing.
- Happy doing.

The boomerang effect: coming back to what you do

In chapter 1, I placed emphasis on how what you actually do makes the difference between being happy and successful or not. I argued that the quality of what you do is determined by the quality of your thinking. In the following three chapters I tried to break open a way of improving the quality of thinking by observing your belief systems and their movement away from threats and toward the rewards. We explored this movement in the context of your self-esteem, need for consistency, your agency, your need to belong and your sense of justice. I then presented the observation about your emotions as messengers and sources of energy to act constructively. Lastly, I tried to open up an alternative way of observing our world.

We now need to conclude as to what we do with this process of thinking about our thinking. I want to do so via an unexpected route. I want you to ask the age old question, "Who am I?"

Of the many different ways this question can be answered, I would like to quote Willem, a friend and colleague. He shared the insight that the only way to answer this question of "Who am I?" satisfactorily is with the answer: "I am in process."

Essentially we are all in the process of dying. From the day we are born, we are on our way to our death. This might sound like a somber note (as it is the last chapter). But death to me is a motivator. Because I know I have an expiry date, I consciously choose to live. Not just survive but thrive. Live to my fullest potential. See if I can maximize the 40% available to me. As one of my clients said, "If death comes, he will have to look for me as I will be busy living."

And that is the point. We are in the process of dying, but the process is living. So who you are is what you are in the process of doing. You are not your work. You are in the process of working. You are not your name; you are in the process of identifying yourself with that name. You are not your thoughts; you are in the process of thinking. You are not your emotions; you are in the process of feeling.

Who you are is what you do. Thoughts, feelings, words are intangible elements of the process. What you do crystallizes everything into reality. So pay attention to what is done, and to what is not done. Not doing is as important as doing.

In life, there are many options. There is much that can keep you busy. But busyness does not create happiness. Your actions must be aligned to your vision. You therefore can choose not to do something in order to create space, spend energy and time on the action that will bring you closer to your dream life. Often ask yourself "What is the alternative here?" "If I did not do this, what could I do instead?"

For example, if I do not watch TV, what could I do instead? Read a book, phone a friend, write down a plan. Which one of these will bring me one step closer to my desired life? Make a choice and do it. Don't underestimate the small things. Nature evolves in incremental changes. Small consistent changes are more sustainable than big radical changes. Just do one thing different each day and see how you build momentum on the way to your life of joy.

The implication of this is that who you are is always in flux. Embrace this. It aligns with the constant change in nature. It proves you are growing. That you are mining the 40% potential available to you.

I hope you enjoyed reading this book as much as I enjoyed writing it. I hope it assisted you in observing your thought process and that it becomes a handy tool in opening up a new potential for happiness and success. Let me know how it goes.

Thank you for joining me sitting in the shade of a tree for a while, out of the burning sun.

Happy doing.

Our Greatest Fear
Our deepest fear is not that we are inadequate.
Our deepest fear is that we are powerful beyond measure.
It is our light, not our darkness that most frightens us.
We ask ourselves, who am I to be brilliant, gorgeous,
talented and fabulous?
Actually, who are you not to be?
You are a child of God.
Your playing small does not serve the world.
There's nothing enlightened about shrinking so that other
people won't feel insecure around you.
We were born to make manifest the glory of
God that is within us.
It's not just in some of us; it's in everyone.
And as we let our own light shine,
we unconsciously give other people
permission to do the same.
As we are liberated from our own fear,
Our presence automatically liberates others.
—Marianne Williamson[39]
(Nelson Mandela used this poem at his inauguration in 1994)

About the Author

Herman Veitch holds a master's degree in Psychology and is an experienced Business, Leadership and Life coach as his professional certified status at the International Coaching Federations testifies.

He lectured in Sports Psychology for six years at the Central University of Technology, Free State, South Africa, and also sat on the research portal of the International Coaching Federation. He was Vice-President of the Bloemfontein Chamber of Commerce and Industry and part of the management team of the Black Managers Forum in Bloemfontein, South Africa. He is a member of a Toastmasters Club and the Mankind Project.

He grew up in Southern Africa and has lived in Belgium and the USA as an adult. He is married to his best friend. He loves exploring and traveling to new places. His hobbies are photography, fencing, horse riding, swimming and aikido.

https://za.linkedin.com/in/hermanveitch

Please be so kind as to leave a review and share your insights.

Join me in the A Space to Think in[1] Facebook group to get updated news about my next planned book: *Thinking About Emotions*

---

1. https://www.facebook.com/groups/876169972534839/

Notes

[1] Something Mihaly Csikszentmihalyi eloquently explains in his book Flow. Another good read is the novel Hector and the Search for Happiness by François Lelord, a French psychiatrist. It tells the story of a psychiatrist (Hector) who travels the world as he attempts to understand "what made people happy." It has sold over two million copies.

[2] Please read Nancy Kline's book, Time to Think, to have a beautiful breakdown of this concept. See Nancy Kline, Time to Think: Listening to Ignite the Human Mind, (1998). London: Cassell. http://www.timetothink.com/book/time-to-think/:

[3] Read Quiet Leadership by David Rock to have a good and useful explanation of how the brain works. See David Rock, Quiet Leadership: Six steps to transforming performance at work, (2006). New York: Collins.

[4] If you are interested in a thorough understanding of these concepts, I cannot recommend enough Thinking, Fast and Slow by Daniel Kahneman. Buy the book. It is worth more than the money you pay. See Daniel Kahneman, Thinking, Fast and Slow, (2011). New York: Farrar, Straus & Giroux.

[5] An entertaining TED video to watch: http://www.ted.com/talks/
peter_doolittle_how_your_working_memory_makes_sense_of_the_wor

[6] Adapted from http://answers.google.com/answers/threadview?id=321024

[7] See Martin Seligman, *Learned Optimism*, (1990). New York: Knopf.

[8] See Martin Seligman, *Authentic Happiness: Using the New Positive Psychology to Realize your Potential for Lasting Fulfillment*, (2002). New York: Free Press.

[9] Don Miguel Ruiz, *The Four Agreements: A Practical Guide to Personal Freedom*, (1997). San Rafael, California: Amber-Allen.

[10] The saying is attributed to Newton. He was using a metaphor which in its earliest known form was attributed to Bernard of Chartres by John of Salisbury. Bernard of Chartres used to say that we [the Moderns] are like dwarves perched on the shoulders of giants [the Ancients], and thus we are able to see more and farther than the latter. And this is not at all because of the acuteness of our sight or the stature of our body, but because. we are carried aloft and elevated by the magnitude of the giants. https://en.wikiquote.org/wiki/Isaac_Newton

[11] I recommend you read it: David Rock, *Your Brain at Work: Strategies for overcoming distraction, regaining focus, and working smarter all day long*, (2009). Harper Business. https://davidrock.net/books/

[12] If you are interested, the book that helped me understand this concept the best is Lynne McTaggart's *The Intention Experiment: Using your Thoughts to Change your Life and the World*, (2007). New York: Simon & Schuster.)

[13] Elizabeth Kübler-Ross wrote a groundbreaking book on these phases. See Kübler-Ross, *On Death and Dying*, (1993). New York: Collier. http://www.ekrfoundation.org/five-stages-of-grief/

[14] My own word. Derived from the word "Iconoclastic" or "Iconoclast" which refers to a person who criticizes or opposes beliefs and practices that are widely accepted; a person who destroys religious images or opposes their veneration. I apply the concept to our ego.

[15] Victor Frankl, *Man's Search for Meaning: An Introduction to Logotherapy*, (1984). New York: Simon & Schuster.

[16] See article I have written for the ICF http://coachfederation.org/about/ article.cfm?ItemNumber=1993&_ga=1.63890858.482002650.13890967738

[17] I highly recommend you read the book *Boundaries* by Dr. Henry Cloud and Dr. John Townsend.

See Henry Cloud & John Townsend, *Boundaries*, (1992). Grand Rapids, Mich: Zondervan.)

[18] In this story line we have different kinds of hero themes. For some it is the conquering hero, some have a tragic hero and some the hidden hero. There is a lot written about the different archetypes people have created through the millenniums. We can find them presented in any play or stage act throughout history.

[19] I first heard this story at a seminar I attended in the 1990s. Not sure who the original author is.

[20]   Helen   Fischer: https://www.youtube.com/watch?v=qv-Jja40ND0

[21]   Harville   Hendrix   -   https://www.youtube.com/watch?v=VD7mQR-ip0Q. See Harville Hendrix, *Getting the Love You Want: A Guide for Couples, (1988).* New York: Holt.

[22] I acknowledge that I am writing from a heterosexual perspective even though the principles discussed here are applicable to all relationship preferences.

[23] Ask Google for one near you.

[24]   https://www.ted.com/talks/robert_waldinger_what_makes_a_good_life_lessons_from_the_longest_s

[25] By Oriah "Mountain Dreamer" House from her book, THE INVITATION © 1999. Published by HarperONE, San Francisco. All rights reserved. Presented with permission of the author. www.oriah.org

[26] http://www.un.org/en/universal-declaration-human-rights/index.html

[27] I recommend you read the work of Piaget and Perry regarding the phases of moral development. And Kohlberg's Stages of Moral Development.

[28]   http://greatergood.berkeley.edu/topic/gratitude____and http://www.dailygood.org/story/578/the-neuroscience-of-why-gratitude-makes-us-healthier-ocean-robbins/

[29] http://academictips.org/blogs/how-the-poor-live/

[30] See Candace Pert, *Molecules of Emotion: Why You Feel the Way You Feel,* (1997). New York: Scribner.

[31] http://www.md-health.com/Parts-Of-The-Brain-And-Function.html

[32] For a more technical point of view have a look at the research done by the Glasgow University: http://www.pnas.org/content/109/19/7241.full#sec-1 or an interpreted version at https://www.aol.com/article/2014/02/07/study-suggests-human-only-have-four-basic-emotions/20825346/

[33] https://www.brainpickings.org/2015/05/15/david-whyte-consolations-anger-forgiveness-maturity/

[34] http://www.indianchild.com/most_beautiful_heart.htm

[35] http://medical-dictionary.thefreedictionary.com/Flow+(psychology)

[36] It was in one of the text books, and I, unfortunately, cannot remember the author.

[37] Koos du Plessis : "Splinterruit" on "Die Vierde Horison" http://www.last.fm/music/Koos+Du+Plessis/_/Splinterruit

[38] There are archetypal patterns that are a set of frequently recurring combinations of growth and balancing structures, and have been widely researched. They have interesting names like Accidental Adversaries, Fixes that Fail, and Tragedy of the Commons. I suggest you explore the archetype further as it falls outside our scope. http://systems-thinking.org/arch/arch.htm

[39] By Marianne Williamson from her book, *A Return to Love,* Reissue edition, (1996). San Francisco: Harper One. Presented with permission of the author. http://marianne.com/a-return-to-love/

Don't miss out!

Visit the website below and you can sign up to receive emails whenever Herman Veitch publishes a new book. There's no charge and no obligation.

https://books2read.com/r/B-A-HPCDB-GTRUC

BOOKS2READ

Connecting independent readers to independent writers.

www.ingramcontent.com/pod-product-compliance
Lightning Source LLC
Chambersburg PA
CBHW031414150726
47989CB00002B/649